20TH CENTURY AMERICAN POP CULTURE

By E. Lee Nelson

1900

On June 1, 1900 the United States population was 76,212,168 people. The average yearly income for a U.S. worker was $432, equal to $11,612 today; the average house cost $5,092, equal to $136,873 today; the average car cost $1,000, equal to $26,880 today; a gallon of gas cost 4 cents, equal to $1.07 today; and a pound of butter cost 25 cents, equal to $6.72 today.

BIRTHS: Travel writer Richard Halliburton (January 9) was lost at sea and presumed dead while attempting to sail a Chinese Junk across the Pacific Ocean in 1939. Actor Spencer Tracy (April 5) was nominated for a record 9 Best Actor Academy Awards, winning 2. Margaret Mitchell (November 8) was an author whose only novel, *Gone With the Wind,* won the 1937 Pulitzer Prize for Fiction. Music composer Aaron Copland (November 14) is known as 'The Dean of American Music Composition.'

ART: The Daniel Webster Memorial statue was dedicated in Washington D.C. on January 19, honoring the U.S. Secretary of State who served under 3 U.S. Presidents. Artist Thomas Eakins created the life size oil painting, *The Thinker: Portrait of Louis N. Kenton,* now on permanent display at New York City's Metropolitan Museum of Art.

FILM: Released on November 16, *The Enchanted Drawing* is a 2-minute silent film that combined animation with live action film. *Sherlock Holmes Baffled* is a 30-second silent film and is the earliest film to feature the famous detective.

INDUSTRY: Harvey Firestone started the Firestone Tire and Rubber Company in Akron, Ohio by supplying tires to original Ford automobiles. The Lionel Corporation, maker of toy trains and model railroads, was founded in New York City. Coleman, the outdoor-recreation and camping gear manufacturer, began when William Coleman started selling kerosene lanterns in Kingfisher, Oklahoma. In February, the Eastman Kodak Company introduced the Brownie Camera for the price of $1. It was a small cardboard box camera that took 2-inch square pictures and helped popularize photography among the general public.

LITERATURE: *The Wonderful Wizard of Oz,* a children's novel written by L. Frank Baum, was originally published on May 17 and sold 21,000 copies in its first year. *Sister Carrie* by Theodore Dreiser has been called 'the greatest American urban novel of all time.'

MUSIC: Popular songs included James Whitcomb Riley's "Shortnin' Bread;" John Philip Sousa's "American Patrol;" Dan Quinn's "Strike Up the Band;" Scott Joplin's "Swipesy;" and Harry Macdonough's "A Bird in a Gilded Cage," which sold over 2 million copies in sheet music. Fritz Scheel founded the Philadelphia Orchestra, serving as its first conductor until his death in 1907.

SPORTS: The first Davis Cup tennis tournament, created by Harvard University tennis player Dwight F. Davis, was played August 8-10 at Longwood Cricket Club in Boston, Massachusetts. The U.S. team defeated the British Isles team 3 matches to 0. The Yale Bulldogs were college football's national champions, going undefeated with a 12-0 record.

THEATRE: Playwright David Belasco's adapted play *Madame Butterfly* premiered March 20 at New York City's Herald Theatre. The musical comedy *San Toy* opened October 10 at Daly's Theatre on Broadway in New York City.

1901

BIRTHS: Inventor Frank Zamboni (January 16) invented the Zamboni Ice Resurfacer, a modified vehicle that transformed the job of resurfacing an ice rink from a 3-man, 90-minute task to a 1-man, 10-minute job. Founder of the Pittsburgh Steelers professional football franchise Art Rooney (January 27) won 4 National Football League Super Bowl championships during the 1970s. Basketball player Chuck Taylor (June 24) teamed with Converse to create the Chuck Taylor All-Star sneaker, the best selling basketball shoe of all time. Cultural anthropologist Margaret Mead (December 16) helped define the 1960s American sexual revolution with her research and writings.

ARCHITECTURE: Philadelphia City Hall is the world's tallest masonry building at 548 feet tall; its weight supported by 22-foot-thick walls at the base. Landmark Center in Saint Paul, Minnesota originally served as the main U.S. Post Office and Courthouse for the state. Frank Lloyd Wright designed Chicago's Willits House, the first building constructed in the famous Prairie House style. The 284 foot tall Soldiers' and Sailors' Monument in Indianapolis, Indiana honors war veterans from the state.

INDUSTRY: Ransom E. Olds developed the modern assembly line to build the first mass produced automobile, the Oldsmobile Curved Dash. K.C. Gillette invented the first safety razor with disposable blades. First year total sales consisted of 51 razors and 168 blades, but by 1904 sales had skyrocketed to 90,000 razors and 123,000 blades. J.P. Morgan founded the world's first billion-dollar corporation, U.S. Steel. Other companies founded in 1901 include Sylvania Electric; Quaker Oats; Texas Fuel Company (Texaco); Dole Foods; Hanes Wear; Nordstrom; Playskool; and Walgreens.

LITERATURE: Mark Twain received an honorary doctor of literature degree from Yale University on October 23. *Selected Poems of Henry Ames Blood* is a collection of 30 poems by the author, chosen by his widow Mary M. Blood. *Up From Slavery* is the autobiography of Booker T. Washington, who details his rise from a poor childhood in slavery to becoming the first president of the Tuskegee Institute in Alabama.

MUSIC: Soprano opera singer Geraldine Farrar made her debut and developed a large following among young women who were nicknamed 'Gerry-flappers.' 1901 popular songs included "I Love You Truly," which has been used at weddings since its release. "Mighty Lak' a Rose" has been covered by Frank Sinatra, Nina Simone, and Jane Powell, among others.

SPORTS: The 8 charter teams of baseball's newest major league, the American League, were: the Baltimore Orioles; the Boston Americans; the Chicago White Stockings; the Cleveland Bluebirds; the Detroit Tigers; the Milwaukee Brewers; the Philadelphia Athletics; and the Washington Senators. The Chicago White Stockings won the American League championship and the Pittsburgh Pirates were National League champions. The New York Yacht Club's *Columbia* defeated the Irish yacht *Shamrock II*, 3 races to 0 in New York City Harbor to retain the America's Cup. Scotland's Willie Anderson won the U.S. Open golf championship at Myopia Hunt Club in South Hamilton, Massachusetts. He was the first golfer to win 4 U.S. Open championships and is still the only man to win 3 consecutive U.S. Open golf titles.

THEATRE: Before his breakthrough story of *Peter Pan,* J.M. Barrie's play *Quality Street* opened on Broadway and ran for only 64 performances.

1902

BIRTHS: Aviator Charles Lindbergh (February 4) became the first person to fly an airplane solo, nonstop across the Atlantic Ocean from New York City to Paris, in 1927. Photographer Ansel Adams (February 20) is famous for his black and white photographs of the American West, especially Yosemite National Park. Author John Steinbeck (February 27) won the 1940 Pulitzer Prize in Fiction for his novel *The Grapes of Wrath*. He also received the Nobel Prize in Literature in 1962. Businessman Ray Kroc (October 5) built McDonald's into the world's most successful fast food restaurant chain.

ARCHITECTURE: The 285 foot tall, 22-story triangular shaped Fuller Building, now known as the Flatiron Building from its resemblance to a clothes iron, opened in New York City at Fifth Avenue and Broadway. America's finest example of Roman Baroque architecture, The Wayne County Building, was completed in Detroit, Michigan.

FILM: Thomas Lincoln Tally opened the Electric Theater, the world's first movie theater, on April 2 in Los Angeles, California. The silent movie *Snow White* made its debut, marking the first time the classic Brothers Grimm fairy tale had been made into a film.

INDUSTRY: Henry Leland founded the oldest American car manufacturer, Cadillac, in Detroit, Michigan. Orville Gibson founded the Gibson Guitar Corporation in Kalamazoo, Michigan. Agricultural machinery maker International Harvester was founded in Canton, Illinois. James Cash Penney founded the J.C. Penney chain of department stores in Kemmerer, Wyoming. Willis Carrier invented modern air conditioning in Buffalo, New York on July 17. Morris and Rose Michtom founded the Ideal Toy Company after they created the Teddy Bear in response to a cartoon depicting President Theodore Roosevelt showing compassion for a bear during a hunting trip in Mississippi.

MUSIC: Popular songs included Edward Elgar's "Land of Hope and Glory;" Paul Lincke's "The Glow Worm;" Theodore Morse's "Happy Hooligan;" Hughie Cannon's "Bill Bailey Won't You Please Come Home;" and "The Entertainer," a classic ragtime two-step written by Scott Joplin and later used as the theme song for the 1973 film *The Sting*.

SPORTS: On January 1 the Michigan Wolverines beat the Stanford Cardinal 49-0 with Stanford quitting in the 3rd quarter, in the first ever college football bowl game at the Rose Bowl in Pasadena, California. Held on Patriots' Day, the third Monday in April, Sammy Mellor won the 6th running of the Boston Marathon in a time of 2:43:12. On April 23, Philadelphia Athletics' infielder Lou Castro of Columbia became the first Latin American born player in Major League Baseball history. Boxer Joe Gans won the World Lightweight Title with a first round knockout of Frank Erne on May 12 in Fort Erie, Ontario, Canada and would successfully defend his title 5 times by the end of the year. *Ring* Magazine rated Gans as the greatest lightweight boxer of all time. Scotland's Laurie Auchterlonie won the U.S. Golf Open at Garden City Golf Club in Garden City, New York. He became the first golfer to score under 80 in all 4 rounds of the U.S. Open.

THEATRE: *The Wizard of Oz* musical premiered in Chicago, Illinois and later moved to Broadway where it ran for 293 performances.

1903

BIRTHS: Ventriloquist Edgar Bergen (February 16) and his dummy Charlie McCarthy were stars of stage and screen for 56 years. His daughter, Candice Bergen, started her acting career as a child on his radio show. Singer Bing Crosby (May 3) recorded the song "White Christmas," written by Irving Berlin, in 1942. It has become the biggest selling single of all time with worldwide sales of 50 million copies. Professional baseball Hall of Fame member Lou Gehrig (June 19) played 17 seasons for the New York Yankees before being stricken with amyotrophic lateral sclerosis (ALS), now commonly known as Lou Gehrig's disease. Caricaturist Al Hirschfeld (June 21) is famous for drawing black and white celebrity portraits, including the cover of rock band Aerosmith's 1977 album *Draw the Line.*

ART: C.M. Coolidge produced several of his 'Dogs Playing Poker' oil paintings, originally commissioned to advertise cigars.

DANCE: Isadora Duncan developed her own style of free dance that became the foundation of American modern dance with her free flowing costumes, bare feet, loose hair, and incorporating the torso much more than in traditional ballet.

FILM: Edwin S. Porter wrote, produced, and directed the first film to use on location shooting, *The Great Train Robbery*; and *Life of an American Fireman,* one of the earliest narrative films. America's first star of the western film genre, Broncho Billy Anderson, made his film debut.

INDUSTRY: Henry Ford founded the Ford Motor Company on June 16 in Detroit, Michigan with $28,000 from 12 investors. David Dunbar Buick created the automobile company Buick in Detroit, Michigan. The Harley Davidson motorcycle manufacturer was founded in Milwaukee, Wisconsin. Pepsi-Cola was invented in New Bern, North Carolina; named from the digestive enzyme pepsin and the kola nuts used in its recipe. The Minnesota Valley Canning Company started in Le Sueur, Minnesota; becoming famous for its canned vegetables and its advertising mascot 'The Jolly Green Giant.'

LITERATURE: Jack London's novella *The Call of the Wild* was originally published in 4 installments by *The Saturday Evening Post* magazine, for which London was paid $750. London then sold all the rights to the story for $2,000 to the publishing company Macmillan, who published it in book form.

MUSIC: Popular songs from 1903 included Arthur Clifford's "In Silence;" Mina Hickman's "Two Eyes of Blue;" Vesta Victoria's "The Country Girl;" John Philip Sousa's "In the Good Old Summer Time;" and Billy Murray's "Up in a Coconut Tree."

SPORTS: Baseball: The first World Series was played between the winners of the American and National leagues with the AL's Boston Americans defeating the NL's Pittsburgh Pirates 5 games to 3 (in a best of nine series). The New York Yankees were founded as the New York Highlanders. The University of Michigan Wolverines (11-0-1) and the Princeton University Tigers (11-0) were college football's co-national champions. Massachusetts-born John Lordan won the Boston Marathon in a time of 2:41:29.

THEATRE: The play *The Pretty Sister of Jose* premiered on Broadway and starred Maude Adams. The musical *Babes in Toyland* opened at the Chicago Grand Opera House before moving to Broadway. Theaters opened: the Colonial Theater in Pittsfield, Massachusetts; the Cutler Majestic Theatre in Boston; and the New Amsterdam Theatre in New York City.

1904

BIRTHS: Gangster Charles Arthur 'Pretty Boy' Floyd (February 3) was named Public Enemy Number One on the FBI's Most Wanted List before being killed by police in 1934. Glenn Miller (March 1) was a music composer and big band leader during the swing era, with hits such as "In the Mood," Chattanooga Choo Choo," and Moonlight Serenade." He disappeared in bad weather over the English Channel and was presumed dead while traveling to entertain U.S. troops in France during World War II. Author and cartoonist Theodor 'Dr. Seuss' Geisel (March 2) created the classic children's books *The Cat in the Hat, Green Eggs and Ham,* and *How the Grinch Stole Christmas!,* among others. Helen Kane (August 4) was a popular singer whose voice and looks were used as the source for the animated cartoon character Betty Boop.

ART: John Singer Sargent, considered one of the greatest portrait painters ever, created the oil on canvas painting, *Mrs. Wertheimer.* The 56-foot tall Vulcan Statue was erected as the city symbol of Birmingham, Alabama and is the world's largest cast iron statue.

INDUSTRY: Motion picture pioneer Marcus Loew founded Loews Theatres in Cincinnati, Ohio by showing short silent films in nickelodeons throughout the East Coast and Midwest states. The candy and chocolate company Brach's Confections was founded in Chicago, Illinois. Its original red brick factory was filmed as part of Gotham Hospital in the 2008 film *The Dark Knight.*

LITERATURE: J.M. Barrie expanded his story of *Peter Pan* into a full-length stage play that would become a Broadway success the following year.

MUSIC: Popular songs included Raymond Browne's "On the Warpath;" Billy Murray's "Meet Me in St. Louis;" Theodore Morse's "Blue Bell;" Hughie Cannon's "He Done Me Wrong;" and Tom Turpin's "Saint Louis Rag."

SPORTS: Baseball: There was no World Series played in 1904 because the National League Champion New York Giants refused to play the American League Champion Boston Americans. Giants' manager John McGraw viewed the AL as a 'junior' or 'minor' league and not worthy of competition. Boston's Cy Young pitched major league baseball's first perfect game on May 5. Football: The University of Michigan Wolverines (10-0), the University of Minnesota Golden Gophers (13-0), and the University of Pennsylvania Quakers (12-0), all shared college football's national championship title. Boxing: Barbados Joe Walcott fought World Light Heavyweight Champion Joe Gans to a 20 round draw in a non-title fight on September 30. Motor Racing: The inaugural Vanderbilt Cup auto race was run over a 30-mile course of winding dirt roads through Nassau County on New York's Long Island and was won by American George Heath, a native Long Islander. The summer Olympics were held in St. Louis, Missouri with the USA winning the most medals (239) and the most gold medals (78).

THEATRE: George M. Cohan's musical, *Little Johnny Jones,* opened at Broadway's Liberty Theater on November 7 and introduced the songs "Give My Regards to Broadway," and "The Yankee Doodle Boy." The Byham Theater opened in Pittsburgh, Pennsylvania on Halloween night, 1904.

1905

BIRTHS: Singer and actor Tex Ritter (January 12) is a member of the Country Music Hall of Fame and is the father of actor John Ritter and the grandfather of actor Jason Ritter. Boxer James J. Braddock (June 7) was the World Heavyweight Champion from 1935 to 1937. Actor Russell Crowe portrayed him in the 2005 film *Cinderella Man*. *Looney Tunes* and *Merry Melodies* cartoon animator and director Friz Freleng (August 21) created the characters of Porky Pig, Tweety Bird, Sylvester the Cat, Yosemite Sam, Speedy Gonzales, and The Pink Panther. Professional women's tennis player Helen Wills Moody (October 6) won 8 Wimbledon singles titles, 7 U.S. Opens, and 4 French Open titles. She also won 2 Olympic gold medals in 1924.

ART & ARCHITECTURE: Photographer Alfred Stieglitz opened the photo art gallery '291' in New York City. It helped gain art photography the same stature as painting and sculpture by exhibiting pioneer art photographers including himself, Edward Steichen, Alvin Langdon Coburn, Gertrude Kasabier, and Clarence H. White. The Gibbes Museum of Art opened in Charleston, South Carolina and features works by local artists Jeremiah Theus, Henrietta Johnston, and Mary Roberts. Frank Lloyd Wright designed the Darwin D. Martin House in Buffalo, New York, which ranks with The Guggenheim Museum in New York City and the Fallingwater House in Pennsylvania as his greatest works.

FILM: Pioneering silent film actor and director Arthur Johnson debuted in the one-reel drama *The White Caps.*

INDUSTRY: Oldsmobile led the world in automobile production, making 6,500 cars, followed by Cadillac at 4,000 cars produced. Spiegel, the mail-order women's clothing and furniture catalog, was first mailed in 1905 and by 1925 had 10 million customers. Claude Hatcher, a pharmacist in Columbus, Georgia, created Royal Crown (RC) cola. The entertainment trade magazine *Variety* was first published, covering the New York vaudeville scene.

LITERATURE: Edith Wharton's novel *The House of Mirth* sold 140,000 copies in the first 3 months after its publication. Mark Twain produced his political satire pamphlet, *King Leopold's Soliloquy.*

MUSIC: Billy Murray's song "In My Merry Oldsmobile" was used by Oldsmobile for several decades as a marketing jingle to sell its cars. The song can be heard playing today on Main Street, USA in Disneyland. Other popular songs included Harry Lauder's "I Love A Lassie;" Leon Jessel's "The Parade Of The Tin Soldiers;" Paul Sarebresole's "Come Clean;" and Bert Williams' "Nobody."

SPORTS: Baseball: The NL's New York Giants defeated the AL's Philadelphia Athletics 4 games to 1 in the World Series. Each of the 5 games was a shutout, with 3 of them won in a 6-day span by Giants' pitcher Christy Mathewson. Football: The University of Chicago Maroons (11-0), and the Yale University Bulldogs (10-0) were college football's co-national champions. Boxing: World Heavyweight Champion James J. Jeffries announced his retirement on May 13 and awarded his title to Marvin Hart after he beat Jack Root in a match refereed by Jeffries in Reno, Nevada on July 3. Golf: Chandler Egan won the U.S. Amateur Golf Championship at the Chicago Golf Club.

THEATRE: The play *The Squaw Man* debuted at Wallack's Theatre on Broadway starring William Faversham and ran for 222 performances.

1906

BIRTHS: Author Robert E. Howard (January 22) is best known for creating the character Conan the Barbarian and is credited with starting the sword and sorcery genre of fantasy fiction. Actor Lon Chaney, Jr. (February 10) portrayed the title role in the 1941 film *The Wolf Man.* Dancer, singer, and actress Josephine Baker (June 3) became the first African American female to star in a major motion picture, 1935's *Princess Tam Tam.* Cosmetics entrepreneur Estee Lauder (July 1) was the only woman on *TIME* magazine's 1998 list of the 20 most influential business geniuses of the 20th century.

ARCHITECTURE: Frank Lloyd Wright designed the Unity Temple in Oak Park, Illinois. It is considered to be the first modern building in the world because of Wright's combination of aesthetics and the use of a single construction material throughout the structure, reinforced concrete.

FILM: Movies released in 1906 include *The Automobile Thieves; Humorous Phases of Funny Faces; The Dream of a Rarebit Fiend; The Merry Frolics of Satan;* and the world's first feature length film, *The Story of the Kelly Gang.*

INDUSTRY: The Kellogg Company was founded in Battle Creek, Michigan after the breakfast cereal Corn Flakes had been invented accidently. Planters snack food company, best known for its processed nuts, was founded in Wilkes-Barre, Pennsylvania.

LITERATURE: Upton Sinclair's novel *The Jungle* was published. Sinclair's portrayal of an immigrant family in Chicago during the early 1900s led to the exposure of poor working conditions in the meatpacking industry. *White Fang* by Jack London was published. Henry Adams wrote his autobiography, *The Education of Henry Adams,* which chronicled his struggles in adapting to the changing 20th century America in his hometown of Boston. *The Spoilers* by Rex Beach, based on a true story of gold prospecting in Alaska, was one of the best-selling novels of 1906.

MUSIC: Popular songs included Charles Zimmerman's U.S. Naval Academy fight song "Anchors Aweigh;" George Cohan's "You're a Grand Old Flag;" Henry Williams' "Cheyenne;" James Scott's "Frog Legs Rag;" and Harry Lauder's "Stop Your Tickling Jock."

SPORTS: Baseball: The AL's Chicago White Sox defeated the NL's Chicago Cubs 4 games to 2 in the World Series. Football: The Princeton University Tigers were college football national champions with a 9-0-1 record. In 1906, a football field was 110 yards in length, kickoffs were made from midfield, touchdowns were worth 5 points and field goals were 4 points. Many new football rule changes were adopted including reducing the length of game from 70 minutes to two 30-minute halves, the offense had to gain 10 yards (instead of 5) in 3 plays for a first down, and the forward pass was made legal for the first time but limited to no more than 20 yards beyond the line of scrimmage and not beyond the goal line (the end zone had not yet been created).

THEATRE: George M. Cohan's musical *Forty-Five Minutes from Broadway* debuted January 1 at the New Amsterdam Theatre in New York City. Victor Herbert's musical *The Red Mill* opened September 24 at Broadway's Knickerbocker Theatre.

1907

BIRTHS: Actress Katharine Hepburn (May 12) enjoyed a career that spanned more than 60 years and is the only woman to win 4 Academy Awards for Best Actress. Professional poker player Johnny Moss (May 14) won the World Series of Poker 3 times, including the inaugural event in 1970. He was one of the charter inductees into the Poker Hall of Fame. Businessman Orville Redenbacher (July 16) created the number one selling brand of popcorn in the U.S. Actor Alan Reed (August 20) is best known for providing the voice of Fred Flintstone on the 1960s animated TV series *The Flintstones*.

ART: *The Steerage* is a photograph taken by Alfred Stieglitz depicting a variety of men and women traveling in the lower-class section of a steamer ship in New York Harbor. It has been hailed as one of the greatest photographs ever taken and is one of the first examples of artistic modernism. The *Rough Rider Monument* in Prescott, Arizona is an equestrian sculpture created by sculptor Solon Borglum.

FILM: Frank Marion founded the Kalem Company in New York City, which produced the first ever film version of *Ben-Hur*. Edwin S. Porter directed the film *Laughing Gas*, which portrays a woman who visits the dentist, receives laughing gas, and continues laughing on her subway ride home, infecting all the other passengers with laughter as well.

INDUSTRY: James E. Casey founded United Parcel Service in Seattle, Washington with $100 borrowed from a friend. Today UPS is the world's largest package delivery company, delivering 15 million packages a day worldwide. The luxury department store chain Neiman Marcus was founded in Dallas, Texas. Henry Goodman started the Goody Hair Product Company by selling rhinestone-studded hair combs from a pushcart.

MUSIC: Popular songs included James Scott's "Kansas City Rag;" Kerry Mills' "Red Wing;" J. Fred Helf's "Tipperay;" George Botsford's "Pride Of The Prairie;" and Edmund Gruber's "The Caisson's Go Rolling Along," which is the official song of the U.S. Army.

SPORTS: Baseball: The NL's Chicago Cubs defeated the AL's Detroit Tigers 4 games to 0, with 1 tie, in the World Series. The first game was called because of darkness and declared a 3-3 tie, the first ever World Series tie game. Football: The Yale University Bulldogs were college football national champions with a record of 9-0-1. Tennis: William Larned defeated Robert LeRoy to win the American Men's Singles Championship and Evelyn Sears beat Carrie Neely to win the Women's Singles Championship at the U.S. Tennis Open in New York City. Golf: Jerome Travers won the U.S. Amateur Golf Championship at Euclid Golf Club in Cleveland, Ohio.

THEATRE: The Ziegfeld Follies were a series of elaborate theatrical productions on Broadway in New York City performed from 1907 through 1931. The Belasco Theatre opened on Broadway featuring Tiffany lighting, ceiling panels, rich woodwork, and expensive murals painted by Everett Shinn. The dome-shaped Foellinger Auditorium was built on the University of Illinois campus in Urbana, Illinois.

1908

BIRTHS: Businessman Frank Stanton (March 20) served as the president of CBS Television from 1946 to 1971. Author Louis L'Amour (March 22) is one of the world's most popular writers of American Old West fiction. Actor and dancer Buddy Ebsen (April 2) performed for 70 years on stage and screen including TV's *The Beverly Hillbillies* and *Barnaby Jones.* Broadcast Journalist Edward R. Murrow (April 25) gave radio news reports during World War II from England beginning with the phrase 'This...is London,' and ending with 'Goodnight, and Good Luck.'

ART & ARCHITECTURE: The Ashcan School was a realist art movement established by a group of artists known as The Eight: William Glackens, Robert Henri, George Luks, John French Sloan, and Everett Shinn. Thomas Eakins produced the oil on canvas painting *William Rush and His Model.* John A. Wilson sculpted the bronze statue *Washington Grays Monument* that stands in Philadelphia's Washington Square and commemorates Pennsylvania volunteer soldiers in the Civil War.

FILM: Popular films were *After Many Years* starring Florence Lawrence; *Dr. Jekyll and Mr. Hyde,* which was the first screen adaptation of Robert Louis Stevenson's novel; the earliest film version of the play *Macbeth;* the first American film version of *Romeo and Juliet;* and *The Thieving Hand,* which is known for its amazing trick photography and special effects for its age. D.W. Griffith made his directorial debut in *The Adventures of Dollie.* Between 1908 and 1913, Griffith directed more than 500 films.

INDUSTRY: General Motors (GM) was formed in Flint, Michigan by incorporating the Oldsmobile and Buick car companies. Fisher Body is an automobile coachbuilder founded by the Fisher brothers in Detroit, Michigan. General Motors' vehicles displayed a 'Body by Fisher' emblem on their door sill plates until the mid-1990s. The first Ford Model T rolled out of the factory at a price of $850. Marquis Mills Converse founded the Converse Rubber Shoe Company in Malden, Massachusetts. James Spangler invented the first portable household vacuum cleaner and founded the Electric Suction Sweeper Company. William Hoover then bought Spangler's patents and created The Hoover Company in Canton, Ohio.

MUSIC: Popular songs included John Philip Sousa's "The Fairest Of The Fair;" Kerry Mills' "Sun Bird;" Ada Jones' "All She Gets from the Iceman Is Ice;" George Botsford's "Black And White Rag;" and Jack Norworth's "Take Me Out to the Ball Game," which has become the unofficial anthem of baseball, sung by fans during the 7th inning stretch at baseball games.

SPORTS: Baseball: The NL's Chicago Cubs defeated the AL's Detroit Tigers 4 games to 1 in the World Series. The Baseball Writers' Association of America was founded on October 14. The group elects players to the Pro Baseball Hall of Fame and selects both leagues' MVP, Cy Young Award winner, and the Rookie and Manager of the Year Award winners each year. Football: The University of Pennsylvania Quakers with an 11-0-1 record and the Harvard University Crimson with a 9-0-1 record were college football co-national champions.

1909

BIRTHS: Drummer and bandleader Gene Krupa (January 15) helped develop modern hi-hat cymbals and tuneable tom-tom drums. He was the first drummer inducted into the Modern Drummer Hall of Fame in 1978. Author Eudora Welty (April 13) won the 1973 Pulitzer Prize for Fiction for her novel *The Optimist's Daughter* and was the first living author to have her works published by the Library of Congress. Architect William Pereira (April 25) had over 400 of his design projects built during his career, most notably the Transamerica Pyramid in San Francisco. Inventor Edwin H. Land (May 7) created 1948's Polaroid instant camera, making it possible to take and develop a picture in less than 60 seconds.

ART & ARCHITECTURE: Realist painter George Bellows, the most acclaimed American artist of the early 20th Century, painted *The Lone Tenement.* Landscape painter Winslow Homer created his last great painting, *Right and Left,* less than 2 years before he died. Sculptor Cyrus Dallin created the bronze equestrian statue, *Appeal to the Great Spirit,* which is owned and displayed by the Boston Museum of Fine Arts. The 15-story, 190-foot tall Stone Place Tower, the first skyscraper built in Dallas, Texas, opened to the public. Frank Lloyd Wright built the greatest example of his Prairie style buildings, the Robie House, in Chicago, Illinois.

FILM: Popular films were *At the Altar,* directed by D.W. Griffith and starring Marion Leonard; *A Corner in Wheat* starring Frank Powell; *The Cowboy Millionaire* starring Tom Mix; the first film version of William Shakespeare's play, *A Midsummer Night's Dream;* and *Mr. Flip,* which featured the first instance of a comedian being hit in the face with a pie. Mary Pickford, Francis Ford (film director John Ford's older brother and mentor), Blanche Sweet, Fatty Arbuckle, and Ethel Clayton made their film debuts.

INDUSTRY: Joseph L. Hudson, founder of Hudson's department store chain, created the Hudson Motor Car Company in Detroit, Michigan. The Manhattan Bridge, connecting Brooklyn to Lower Manhattan in New York City, opened to traffic on December 31. The U.S. Army Signal Corps paid the Wright Brothers $30,000 (equal to $776,000 today) for their Wright Military Flyer, an airplane capable of flying 2 people at a speed of 40 miles per hour for a distance of 125 miles. Pearson's Candy Company, makers of the Nut Goodie and Salted Nut Roll candy bars, was founded in Saint Paul, Minnesota.

MUSIC: Popular songs included Robert Hoffman's "I'm Alabama Bound;" Billy Murray's "By The Light of the Silvery Moon;" Ada Jones' "The Yama Yama Man;" the Fisk Jubilee Singers' "Swing Low, Sweet Chariot;" and Charles Wakefield Cadman's "From the Land of Sky-Blue Water," later used by Hamm's Beer for its advertising jingle.

SPORTS: Baseball: The NL's Pittsburgh Pirates defeated the AL's Detroit Tigers 4 games to 3 in the World Series. Football: The Yale University Bulldogs were college football national champions with a 10-0 record. Motor Racing: The Indianapolis Motor Speedway in Indiana opened on August 14 with 7 motorcycle races. Harry Grant, driving an ALCO-Berliet racecar, won the 5th running of the Vanderbilt Cup auto race on New York's Long Island.

THEATRE: The theatrical version of the children's novel, *Rebecca of Sunnybrook Farm,* debuted on Broadway. Theaters opened: San Francisco's Roxie Theater and Seattle's Nippon Kan Theatre.

1910

On April 15, the U.S. population was 92,228,496 people. The average yearly income for a U.S. worker was $538, equal to $12,781 today; the average house cost $5,848, equal to $138,932 today; the average car cost $950, equal to $22,569 today; a gallon of gas cost 7 cents, equal to $1.66 today; and a loaf of bread and a quart of milk cost 3 cents each, equal to 71 cents each today.

BIRTHS: Actress Gloria Stuart (July 4) was the oldest person to be nominated for an Academy Award, at the age of 87 for her role as the elderly Rose Dawson in the 1997 film *Titanic.* Artist Dorothea Tanning (August 25) was a painter, sculptor, writer, and designer of sets and costumes for ballet and theater. Architectural photographer Julius Shulman (October 10) helped promote mid-century modern design through his photographs. Record producer John Hammond (December 15) started or furthered the recording careers of Benny Goodman, Billie Holiday, Count Basie, Pete Seeger, Aretha Franklin, Bob Dylan, Bruce Springsteen, and Stevie Ray Vaughan.

FILM: Popular films were *Hamlet; Frankenstein; A Christmas Carol; Alice's Adventures in Wonderland;* and *The Wonderful Wizard of Oz. In Old California* was the first movie to be filmed in Hollywood. Known as 'The Biograph Girl,' actress Florence Lawrence became the world's first movie star, appearing in nearly 50 films in 1910. Tom Mix, Norma Talmadge, Wallace Reid, Mae Marsh, and Pearl White made their film debuts.

INDUSTRY: Chicago publisher William Boyce founded the Boy Scouts of America in Irving, Texas on February 8. Philip Parmelee piloted the first commercial cargo flight 65 miles from Dayton, Ohio to Columbus, Ohio, carrying 100 pounds of silk valued at $1,000 for the opening of a department store. Businessman Joyce Hall founded Hallmark Cards in Kansas City, Missouri, which grew into the world's largest maker of greeting cards. The Ford Motor Company sold 10,000 Model T cars at a price of $950.

LITERATURE: Works published include *The Emerald City of Oz* and *Aunt Jane's Nieces in Society* by L. Frank Baum, *Heritage of the Desert* by Zane Grey, and Franklin Peirce Adams' poem "Baseball's Sad Lexicon," which contained the popular refrain, 'Tinker to Evers to Chance.' Mark Twain died on April 21, the day after Halley's Comet appeared, exactly 74 years after its previous visit on the day Twain was born.

MUSIC: Popular songs included Blanche Ring's "Come Josephine in My Flying Machine;" Tell Taylor's "Down by The Old Mill Stream;" Charles Johnson's "Silver Star;" Sophie Tucker's "Some of These Days;" and The Peerless Quartet's "Let Me Call You Sweetheart."

SPORTS: Baseball: The AL's Philadelphia Athletics defeated the NL's Chicago Cubs 4 games to 1 in the World Series. Football: The Harvard University Crimson were college football's national champions with a record of 8-0-1. A new football rule stated that a receiver could not be interfered with until the ball was caught. In boxing's first 'Fight of the Century,' African-American Jack Johnson defeated 'The Great White Hope' James Jeffries in round 15 to retain his World Heavyweight Championship Title, sparking race riots across the U.S.

1911

BIRTHS: Playwright Tennessee Williams (March 26) won 2 Pulitzer Prizes for Drama, for *A Streetcar Named Desire* in 1948 and *Cat on a Hot Tin Roof* in 1955. He also received the Presidential Medal of Freedom in 1980. Blues musician Robert Johnson (May 8) is known as the father of 'Mississippi Delta Blues' by influencing countless guitar players. Athlete Babe Zaharias (June 26) won 48 professional golf tournaments and two 1932 Olympic Gold Medals, in the 80 meter hurdles and the javelin throw, during her career. Actress Lucille Ball (August 6) starred in the 1950s TV sitcom *I Love Lucy* and became the first woman to run a major TV studio, Desilu, which produced many popular TV series including *Star Trek; Hogan's Heroes; The Andy Griffith Show; Mission Impossible; Family Affair; That Girl;* and *Mannix*.

ARCHITECTURE: The main branch of the New York Public Library officially opened on May 23 at a construction cost of $9 million and an initial collection consisting of more than 1,000,000 volumes. Architect Frank Lloyd Wright built his summer home and studio, Taliesin, near Spring Green, Wisconsin. The Triangle Shirtwaist Factory fire, which killed 146 workers, led to improved safety standards in New York City buildings.

FILM: Popular films were *The Battle; The Cowboy and the Lady; His Trust; David Copperfield;* and *The Lonedale Operator* (in which director D.W. Griffith is credited with using the first close-up shot in film history). David Horsley opened Nestor Studios, the first movie studio located in Hollywood, California. Lionel Barrymore, Lillian Russell, Alan Hale, Sr., Lois Weber, and Harold Lockwood made their film debuts.

INDUSTRY: Louis Chevrolet founded Chevrolet Automobiles in Detroit, Michigan on November 3 to directly compete against the Ford Motor Company. The Whirlpool Corporation was founded in St. Joseph, Michigan and is now the world's largest maker of home appliances. Candy maker Mars, Inc. was founded in Tacoma, Washington and is now the 5th largest privately held company in the U.S. with 70,000 employees.

MUSIC: Popular songs included Irving Berlin's "Alexander's Ragtime Band;" Billy Murray's "On Moonlight Bay" and "Any Little Girl, That's a Nice Little Girl, is the Right Little Girl For Me;" Nora Bayes' "Turn Off Your Light, Mr. Moon Man;" and Harry Lauder's "Roamin' In The Gloamin'."

SPORTS: Baseball: The AL's Philadelphia Athletics defeated the NL's New York Giants 4 games to 2 in the World Series. Baseball's first Most Valuable Player awards were presented as the Chalmers Award to the AL's Ty Cobb of the Detroit Tigers and to the NL's Frank Schulte of the Chicago Cubs. Football: The Princeton University Tigers were college football national champions with a record of 8-0-2. Motor Racing: Ray Harroun won the first Indianapolis 500 in a Marmon Automobile racecar nicknamed the 'Wasp' that featured the earliest known rear-view mirror mounted on a motor vehicle.

THEATRE: Mary Hunter Austin's play about American Indian life, *The Arrow Maker,* was first presented at the New Theatre in New York City. C.M.S. McLellan's play, *Marriage a la Carte,* opened January 2 at Broadway's Casino Theatre. The musical *The Siren* ran for 116 performances at the Knickerbocker Theatre in New York City. Theaters opened: The Frances Building and Echo Theater in Portland, Oregon; Robey Theatre in Spencer, West Virginia; and Tappan Zee Playhouse in Nyack, New York.

1912

BIRTHS: Artist Jackson Pollock (January 28) was a leader in mid century abstract expressionism, best known for his unique style of drip painting. Professional golfers Byron Nelson (February 4), who won 11 consecutive tournaments in 1945; Sam Snead (May 27), who won a record 82 PGA Tour titles; and Ben Hogan (August 13), who won 9 major championship titles with what many consider the best golf swing ever. Fashion editor Sally Kirkland (July 1) was the only fashion editor at *LIFE* magazine for 25 years and helped make Grace Kelly, Audrey Hepburn, and Jacqueline Kennedy Onassis fashion icons. Actress and dancer Eleanor Powell (November 21) is known as 'the world's greatest tap dancer' from the 1930s.

ART & ARCHITECTURE: Portraitist Lydia Field Emmet, whose paintings hang in the White House, New York City's Metropolitan Museum of Art, and Washington D.C's National Gallery of Art, painted her self portrait. The major league baseball stadiums Fenway Park, home to the Boston Red Sox, and Tiger Stadium, home to the Detroit Tigers, both opened on April 20 with 11 inning victories for the home teams.

FILM: Popular films were *Cleopatra* starring Helen Gardner; *For His Son* starring Blanche Sweet; *Custer's Last Fight* starring Francis Ford; *The Honor of the Family* starring Lon Chaney, Sr. in his first film role; and the first gangster film in history, *The Musketeers of Pig Alley*. Actor and director Mack Sennett, creator of slapstick comedy in film, founded Keystone Studios in Los Angeles, California. Carl Laemmle founded the oldest movie studio in the U.S., Universal Studios, in New York City. Adolph Zukor founded Paramount Pictures, which is the last major film studio still headquartered in Hollywood.

INDUSTRY: Leon Leonwood Bean founded the clothing and outdoor equipment retailer L.L. Bean Company in Freeport, Maine when he created a waterproof boot that he sold to hunters through the mail. Juliette Gordon Low founded the Girl Scouts of America in Savannah, Georgia on March 12. The Roman Meal bread company was founded in Tacoma, Washington.

LITERATURE: Edgar Rice Burroughs' novel *Tarzan of the Apes* was first published in the pulp magazine *All-Story Magazine.* The character became so popular that Burroughs wrote a further 24 Tarzan sequels into the 1940s.

MUSIC: Popular songs included Ernest Ball's "When Irish Eyes Are Smiling;" "My Melancholy Baby" by William Frawley (who later played Fred Mertz on TV's *I Love Lucy);* Bob Roberts' "Ragtime Cowboy Joe;" and W.C. Handy's "The Memphis Blues," which became one of the first hit blues songs.

SPORTS: Baseball: The AL's Boston Red Sox defeated the NL's New York Giants 4 games to 3 in the World Series with a 3-2, 10th inning walk-off victory in the final game. Football: The Harvard University Crimson were college football national champions with a 9-0 record in the first season of the modern era. New rule changes included: teams having 4 downs instead of 3 to gain 10 yards, touchdowns were worth 6 points instead of 5, the field was reduced from 110 yards to 100, with 10 yard end zones added, and kickoffs were made from the 40 yard line rather than midfield.

THEATRE: The 'Little Theatre Movement' developed new theatrical performance styles in Chicago, Boston, Seattle, and Detroit to combat the rising popularity of cinema.

1913

BIRTHS: Sportscaster Mel Allen (February 14) was the radio and TV announcer for the New York Yankees from 1939 to 1964 and also called 22 World Series and 24 All-Star Games. He was the host of TV's *This Week in Baseball* from 1977 to 1996. Legendary football coaches Vince Lombardi (June 11) led the Green Bay Packers to 5 NFL titles in the 1960s including the first 2 Super Bowls; and Paul 'Bear' Bryant (September 11), who won 6 National Championships at the University of Alabama during his 25 year coaching career. Winemaker Robert Mondavi (June 18) helped bring worldwide recognition to the wines of California's Napa Valley.

ART & ARCHITECTURE: The Armory Show opened in New York City on February 17, introducing modern art paintings such as *Cliff Dwellers* by George Bellows. Sculptor James Earle Fraser designed the Indian Head (Buffalo) nickel coin. New York City's Grand Central Terminal was rebuilt, and re-opened on February 1 as the world's largest train station. The Woolworth Building opened April 24 in New York City and remains, at 57 stories and 792 feet tall, one of the 20 tallest buildings in New York. Ebbets Field, the home park of Major League Baseball's Brooklyn Dodgers, opened April 9 in Brooklyn, New York.

FILM: Popular films were *The Unwelcome Guest* starring Mary Pickford; *Some Fools There Were* starring William Garwood; *The Spender* starring Florence Lawrence; *The Battle of Gettysburg,* which was filmed in Malibu, California; and the first werewolf movie ever made, *The Werewolf*, starring Clarence Burton. Charlie Chaplin signed a contract on December 29 with Mack Sennett to begin making films at Keystone Studios. Harold Lloyd, Gladys Brockwell, and Wallace Beery made their film debuts.

INDUSTRY: The R.J. Reynolds Tobacco Company introduced Camel, the first packaged cigarette. The Ford Motor Company developed the first moving assembly line, which reduced chassis assembly time from 12.5 hours to 2.5 hours and created an era of mass production in the U.S.

LITERATURE: Works published include Eleanor Porter's *Pollyanna;* Jack London's *The Valley of the Moon;* Ellen Glasgow's *Virginia;* Edith Wharton's *The Custom of the Country;* and Willa Cather's *O Pioneers!*

MUSIC: Popular songs included Frederick Weatherly's "Danny Boy;" Irving Berlin's "San Francisco Bound;" Fred Fisher's "Peg O' My Heart;" Harry Carroll's "The Trail Of The Lonesome Pine;" and James Monaco's "You Made Me Love You (I Didn't Want To Do It)."

SPORTS: Baseball: The AL's Philadelphia Athletics defeated the NL's New York Giants 4 games to 1 in the World Series. Football: The University of Chicago Maroons with a 7-0 record and the Harvard University Crimson with a 9-0 record were college football co-national champions. Golf: Francis Ouimet became the first amateur to win the U.S. Open golf championship with a surprising playoff victory over Harry Vardon and Ted Ray at The Country Club in Brookline, Massachusetts.

THEATRE: L.Frank Baum's musical *The Tik-Tok Man of Oz* opened in Los Angeles, California on March 31. Theaters opened: Boston's Wilbur Theatre and the Park Theatre in Estes Park, Colorado, which is the oldest operating cinema in the western U.S.

1914

BIRTHS: Author William S. Burroughs (February 5) was a leading figure in the Beat Generation and is best known for his 1959 novel *Naked Lunch*. Boxer Joe Louis (May 13) was the World Heavyweight Champion from 1937 to 1949, during which time he successfully defended his title a record 25 times. Dancer and choreographer Frankie Manning (May 26) was one of the original creators of the Lindy Hop dance in the late 1920s. Graphic designer Paul Rand (August 15) is best known for designing the corporate logos for IBM, ABC, UPS, and Westinghouse.

ART & ARCHITECTURE: Modernist painter Marsden Hartley painted the *Portrait of a German Officer*. Sculptor Evelyn Beatrice Longman created the 16-ton, 24-foot tall bronze statue *Spirit of Communication* as the symbol of the telecommunications corporation AT&T. It is on display at its corporate headquarters in Dallas, Texas. Wrigley Field, home to Major League Baseball's Chicago Cubs, opened on April 23. After 33 years of construction, the Panama Canal opened on August 15, making it possible to travel between the Atlantic and Pacific Oceans in half the time previously required.

FILM: Popular films were *Cinderella* starring Mary Pickford; *Brewster's Millions* starring Edward Abeles; *The Million Dollar Mystery* starring Florence La Badie; *The Squaw Man* featuring Cecil B. DeMille in his directorial debut; and *Making a Living* starring Charlie Chaplin in his first film. Rudolph Valentino, John and Ethel Barrymore, Gloria Swanson, and Oliver Hardy also made their film debuts in 1914.

INDUSTRY: Horace and John Dodge founded the Dodge automobile company in Detroit, Michigan. John D. Hertz founded the taxi service, Yellow Cab Company, in Chicago, Illinois. Greyhound Bus Lines started in Hibbing, Minnesota. The Toro Company, makers of lawn maintenance and snow removal equipment, was founded in Bloomington, Minnesota. The Chicken of the Sea canned tuna company was founded in San Diego, California.

MUSIC: Popular songs included Arthur Fields' "The Aba Daba Honeymoon;" Jean Schwartz's "Chinatown, My Chinatown;" W.C. Handy's "St. Louis Blues;" Irving Berlin's "Follow The Crowd;" Ray Gilbert's "That's a Plenty;" and Jerome Kern's "They Didn't Believe Me."

SPORTS: Baseball: The NL's Boston Braves swept the AL's Philadelphia Athletics 4 games to 0 to win the World Series. Babe Ruth played in his first major league baseball game, debuting as a pitcher for the Boston Red Sox on July 11 and defeating the Cleveland Indians 4-3. Football: The University of Illinois Fighting Illini were college football national champions with a record of 7-0. Boxing: Future World Heavyweight Champion Jack Dempsey fought his first match, a 6-round draw against Young Herman on August 17 in Ramona, Colorado. Golf: Walter Hagen won the first of his 2 U.S. Open golf championships at the Midlothian Country Club in Midlothian, Illinois. Motor Racing: Ralph DePalma won the Vanderbilt Cup auto race in Santa Monica, California.

THEATRE: The Mark Strand Movie Theatre was built in New York City's Times Square with a seating capacity of 3,300 people at a cost of $1 million. Known as the 'Apollo Theatre of the South,' the Attucks Theatre was designed, financed, and constructed by African American entrepreneurs in Norfolk, Virginia.

1915

BIRTHS: Actor Orson Welles (May 6) wrote, produced, directed, and starred in his first film, 1941's *Citizen Kane,* which many critics consider the greatest film ever made. Flautist Julius Baker (September 23) was the principal flute player for the New York Philharmonic for 18 years and taught flute at the Juilliard School in New York City. Playwright Arthur Miller (October 17) wrote *Death of a Salesman,* which won the 1949 Pulitzer Prize for Drama and Tony Award for Best Play. He was married to Actress Marilyn Monroe from 1956 to 1961. Comic Book Writer Bob Kane (October 24) created the DC Comics superhero Batman in 1939.

ART: Sculptor Cyrus Dallin created the bronze statue *The Scout,* which depicts a Sioux Indian on horseback overlooking downtown Kansas City, Missouri. It inspired the name and served as the team logo for the National Hockey League's Kansas City Scouts. The women's fashion magazine *Harper's Bazaar* hired artist Romain Tirtoff to design its covers.

FILM: Popular films were D.W. Griffith's 3 hour and 10 minute epic *The Birth of a Nation* starring Lillian Gish; *Burlesque on Carmen* starring Charlie Chaplin; *The Cheat* directed by Cecil B. DeMille and starring Fannie Ward in her film debut; *A Fool There Was* starring Theda Bara; and *Fatty's Tintype Tangle* directed by and starring Fatty Arbuckle. The film *Inspiration* featured the first nude scene by a leading actress, Audrey Munson. W.C. Fields, Mary Boland, Douglas Fairbanks, Geraldine Farrar, Laura Hope Crews, Pauline Frederick, Charlotte Greenwood, and Edna Perviance made their film debuts.

INDUSTRY: New York City chemist T.L. Williams founded the Maybelline cosmetics company after noticing his younger sister Maybel applying a mixture of Vaseline and coal dust to her eyelashes. Willis Carrier started the Carrier air conditioning company in Newark, New Jersey. North America's second largest supermarket chain, Safeway, was founded in Pocatello, Idaho. Community service group Kiwanis International was founded in Detroit, Michigan. William F. O'Neil founded the General Tire and Rubber Company in Akron, Ohio.

MUSIC: Popular songs included Alma Gluck's "Carry Me Back To Old Virginny;" Morton Harvey's "I Didn't Raise My Boy to be a Soldier;" Joe Cooper's "I've Been Floating Down the Old Green River;" Henry Cohan's "Canadian Capers;" and George L. Cobb's "Alabama Jubilee."

SPORTS: Baseball: The AL's Boston Red Sox defeated the NL's Philadelphia Phillies 4 games to 1 in the World Series. New York Yankees pitcher Jack Warhop gave up Babe Ruth's first career home run on May 6 while Ruth was playing for the Boston Red Sox. Football: The Cornell University Big Red with a 9-0 record and the University of Pittsburgh Panthers at 8-0 were college football co-national champions. Boxing: Jess Willard defeated Jack Johnson with a 26th round knockout to become World Heavyweight Champion in Havana, Cuba.

THEATRE: Jerome Kern's musical *Very Good Eddie* ran on Broadway for 341 performances. Irving Berlin's musical *Stop! Look! Listen!* opened on Broadway at the Globe Theatre on Christmas Day and ran for 105 performances. Theaters opened: Boston's Fenway Theatre; Detroit's Majestic Theater; the Hippodrome Theatre in Terre Haute, Indiana; Pittsburgh's Garden Theater; and the Al Ringling Theatre in Baraboo, Wisconsin.

1916

BIRTHS: Dinah Shore (February 29) was a singer, actress, and TV personality who charted 80 popular hit songs from 1940 to 1959. Television producer Sherwood Schwartz (November 14) created the TV series *Gilligan's Island* in 1964 and *The Brady Bunch* in 1969. Actor Kirk Douglas (December 9) is best known for portraying the title role in the 1960 film *Spartacus.* Betty Grable (December 18) was an actress, dancer, and singer whose iconic World War II era pin-up girl poster was included in *Life* magazine's '100 Photos that Changed the World.'

ART: After 8 years of work, sculptor Paul Wayland Bartlett completed his masterpiece, *The Apotheosis of Democracy,* a marble pediment sculpture on the U.S. Capitol House of Representatives in Washington, D.C. Norman Rockwell's painting *Boy With Baby Carriage* became his first cover for the *Saturday Evening Post* magazine on May 20.

FILM: Popular films were *Intolerance* starring Lillian Gish; *20,000 Leagues Under the Sea; Snow White* starring Marguerite Clark; *Under Two Flags* starring Theda Bara; and *The Americano* starring Douglas Fairbanks. Billie Burke, Edward G. Robinson, and Mae Murray made their film debuts.

INDUSTRY: Automobile maker Nash Motors was founded in Kenosha, Wisconsin by former General Motors president Charles Nash. William Boeing started the aircraft manufacturer The Boeing Company in Seattle, Washington, which has grown to become the largest exporter by revenue in the U.S. The Curtiss Candy Company, makers of such candy bars as Baby Ruth and Butterfinger, was created in Chicago, Illinois. The supermarket chain Piggly Wiggly, the first self-service grocery store, was founded in Memphis, Tennessee. The children's toy Lincoln Logs were invented by John Lloyd Wright, son of architect Frank Lloyd Wright.

MUSIC: Popular songs included W. C. Handy's "Beale Street Blues;" Spencer Williams' "I Ain't Got Nobody;" Enrico Caruso's "O Sole Mio;" Billy Murray's "Pretty Baby;" and James Harrison's "Keep the Home Fires Burning."

SPORTS: Baseball: The AL's Boston Red Sox defeated the NL's Brooklyn Dodgers 4 games to 1 in the World Series. Football: The University of Pittsburgh Panthers were college football national champions with an 8-0 record under coach Pop Warner. Hockey: The Portland Rosebuds became the first U.S. team to win the Pacific Coast Hockey Association Championship. Golf: Chick Evans won both the U.S. Open championship at the Minikahda Club in Minneapolis, Minnesota and the U.S. Amateur championship at Merion Golf Club in Ardmore, Pennsylvania. Jim Barnes won the first USPGA golf championship, played at that time in match play format, at Siwanoy Country Club in Eastchester, New York.

THEATRE: The musical *Robinson Crusoe, Jr.* starring Al Jolson premiered at Broadway's Winter Garden Theatre and ran for 139 performances. Cole Porter's first Broadway production, *See America First,* was a critical and commercial flop. The Coliseum Theater in Seattle, Washington opened as the world's first cinema palace featuring a 7-piece orchestra plus an organist. It continued to show movies until 1995, when it was converted into a Banana Republic clothing store.

1917

BIRTHS: Writer Sidney Sheldon (February 11) created the TV series *The Patty Duke Show* in 1963, *I Dream of Jeannie* in 1965, and *Hart to Hart* in 1979. He also wrote thriller novels such as *The Other Side of Midnight, Rage of Angels,* and *Master of the Game,* which helped him become the seventh best selling writer of all time. Cartoonist Will Eisner (March 6) created the masked crime fighter *The Spirit* in 1940. Vocalist Ella Fitzgerald (April 25) won 13 Grammy Awards, the National Medal of Arts, and the Presidential Medal of Freedom during her 59-year recording career. Publisher Katherine Graham (June 16) led the *Washington Post* newspaper from 1963 to 1991. Her autobiography, *Personal History,* won the Pulitzer Prize in 1998.

FILM: Popular films were *Joan the Woman,* directed by Cecil B. DeMille and starring Geraldine Farrar as Joan of Arc; *The Little American,* directed by DeMille and starring Mary Pickford; *The Butcher Boy* starring Fatty Arbuckle and Buster Keaton in his film debut; *Easy Street* starring Charlie Chaplin and Edna Purviance; and *The Tornado,* with John Ford in his directorial debut. Marion Davies, Stan Laurel, ZaSu Pitts, Bela Lugosi, Richard Dix, and Loretta Young made their film debuts.

INDUSTRY: The Radio Flyer toy wagon company was founded in Chicago, Illinois. Henry Leland created the Lincoln Car Company in Detroit, Michigan. The Falstaff Brewing Company, maker of Falstaff Beer, was founded in St. Louis, Missouri. Magnavox (Latin for 'great voice') Electronics Corporation was founded in Napa, California. The Phillips Petroleum Company, famous for its Phillips 66 gas and service stations, was created in Bartlesville, Oklahoma. Direct mail order marketer of meat, Omaha Steaks, started as a single butcher shop in Omaha, Nebraska. Sunsweet Growers, the world's largest producer of dried fruits, was founded in Yuba City, California.

LITERATURE: The first Pulitzer Prizes were awarded with Jean Jules Jusserand receiving the first Pulitzer for History for his work *With Americans of Past and Present Days,* and Herbert B. Swope receiving the first Pulitzer for Journalism for his reporting work for the *New York World* newspaper. Sinclair Lewis' novel, *The Job*, drew attention to the rights of working women. Edith Wharton's novel, *Summer,* was published.

MUSIC: Popular songs included the first jazz recording ever released, "Livery Stable Blues" by The Original Dixieland Jass Band; Nora Bayes' "Over There;" George Meyer's "For Me And My Gal;" Douglas Furber's "The Bells of St. Mary's;" and Joseph McCarthy's "I'm Always Chasing Rainbows."

SPORTS: Baseball: The AL's Chicago White Sox defeated the NL's New York Giants 4 games to 2 in the World Series. Football: The Georgia Institute of Technology Yellow Jackets were college football national champions with a 9-0 record under coach John Heisman. Hockey: The Seattle Metropolitans became the first U.S. team to win the Stanley Cup when they defeated the Montreal Canadiens 3 games to 1.

THEATRE: Jesse Lynch Williams' play *Why Marry?* won the first Pulitzer prize for Drama.

1918

BIRTHS: Entrepreneur Sam Walton (March 29) founded the retail store chains Walmart in 1962 and Sam's Club in 1983. Ted Williams (August 30) was the last player in Major League Baseball to bat over .400 in a single season (.406 in 1941) and reached base 48 percent of the time over his 22-year career with the Boston Red Sox. Radio broadcaster Paul Harvey (September 4) had a listening audience of 24 million people each week on 1,200 radio stations. Theater producer, director, and choreographer Jerome Robbins (October 11) was a five-time Tony Award winner who also won the Best Director Academy Award for the 1961 film *West Side Story.*

ART: Eric Enstrom's photograph, *Grace,* depicts an elderly man seated at a table with hands folded, saying a prayer with a simple meal.

FILM: Popular films were *Mickey* starring Mabel Normand; the first Tarzan movie ever made, *Tarzan of the Apes; Arizona* starring Douglas Fairbanks; *Shoulder Arms* directed by and starring Charlie Chaplin; and *Hearts of the World* starring Lillian and Dorothy Gish and directed by D.W. Griffith. Warner Bros. Pictures was established when brothers Harry, Albert, Sam, and Jack Warner opened their first film studio on Hollywood's Sunset Boulevard. Will Rogers made his film debut, later becoming the highest-paid movie star of the 1920s and 30s.

INDUSTRY: Zenith Electronics Corporation, which produced the modern wireless TV remote control and the first company to develop HDTV in North America, was founded in Chicago, Illinois. Dickies, manufacturer of work-related clothing, was created in Bryan, Texas. The Hertz car rental company started in Chicago, Illinois with 12 Ford Model T cars. Benjamin Ritz founded Ritz Camera Centers as a portrait studio in the Ritz Hotel in Atlantic City, New Jersey. Lysol disinfectant was created as a countermeasure to the Spanish Flu virus. Velveeta processed cheese product was invented in Monroe, New York.

LITERATURE: Ernest Poole' *His Family* received the first Pulitzer Prize for the Novel. Willa Cather published the final book of her 'Prairie Trilogy' novels, *My Antonia,* succeeding *O Pioneers!* and *The Song of the Lark.*

MUSIC: Popular songs included Turner Layton's "After You've Gone;" Leo Wood's "Somebody Stole My Gal;" Richard Whiting's "Till We Meet Again;" The Original Dixieland Jass Band's "Tiger Rag;" and Bob Carleton's Ja-Da." Irving Berlin wrote the patriotic song, "God Bless America" while serving in the U.S. Army at Camp Upton in Yaphank, New York.

SPORTS: Baseball: The AL's Boston Red Sox defeated the NL's Chicago Cubs 4 games to 2 in the World Series. Babe Ruth of the Red Sox led the American League in home runs for the first time, hitting 11. Football: Most professional teams shut down due to World War I and the Spanish flu pandemic. The University of Michigan Wolverines with a 5-0 record and the University of Pittsburgh Panthers with a 4-1 record were college football co-national champions.

THEATRE: Jerome Kern's musical *Oh, Lady! Lady!!* premiered at Broadway's Princess Theatre and ran for 219 performances. The Stephen Sondheim Theatre, formerly Henry Miller's Theatre, opened on Broadway as the first air-conditioned theater in Manhattan.

1919

BIRTHS: Writer J.D. Salinger (January 1) is best known for his only novel, *The Catcher in the Rye,* published in 1951, and his reclusive lifestyle. Jackie Robinson (January 31) became the first black Major League Baseball player when he debuted with the Brooklyn Dodgers in 1947. Folk musician, songwriter, and activist Pete Seeger (May 3) has enjoyed a career that has spanned over 73 years. Kitty Wells (August 30) became the first female country music singer to top the U.S. country charts with her 1952 hit single "It Wasn't God Who Made Honky Tonk Angels."

ART & ARCHITECTURE: John Singer Sargent painted the 8-by-20 foot *Gassed,* an oil painting depicting the aftermath of a mustard gas attack during World War I. Virginia's Newport News Victory Arch monument was erected. The Newby-McMahon Building, known as the world's smallest skyscraper, was built in Wichita Falls, Texas.

FILM: Popular films were *The Miracle Man* starring Lon Chaney; *Male and Female* starring Gloria Swanson and directed by Cecil B. DeMille; *When the Clouds Roll By* starring Douglas Fairbanks; *True Heart Susie* starring Lilian Gish; and *The Delicious Little Devil* starring Rudolph Valentino. Charlie Chaplin, Mary Pickford, D.W. Griffith, and Douglas Fairbanks created United Artists Film Studio to better control their films profits. Boris Karloff, Fay Wray, Shemp Howard, Norma Shearer, and the first ever cartoon character, Felix the Cat, made their film debuts.

INDUSTRY: The electronics company Radio Corporation of America (RCA) was formed in New York City by General Electric, Westinghouse, and others. Cummins Engine Company was founded in Columbus, Indiana. Today it is the world's largest producer of diesel technology, powering vehicles made by Ford, Dodge RAM, Case IH, Freightliner, Peterbilt, and Kenworth. Conrad Hilton founded Hilton Hotels, which grew to become the first nationwide hotel chain across the U.S. The hamburger and root beer restaurant chain A&W was founded in Lodi, California. Bubble Up, the lemon-lime soda, was created in Sandusky, Ohio.

LITERATURE: Booth Tarkington's *The Magnificent Ambersons* won the Pulitzer Prize for the Novel.

MUSIC: Popular songs were Al Jolson's "Swanee" and "You Ain't Heard Nothing Yet;" Irving Berlin's "Mandy;" Ben Selvin's "I'm Forever Blowing Bubbles;" and Clarence Williams' "Baby, Won't You Please Come Home?"

SPORTS: Baseball: The NL's Cincinnati Red defeated the AL's Chicago White Sox 5 games to 3 in the World Series (in a short return to the best of 9 series format). Eight members of the White Sox were banned for life from baseball for intentionally losing games in the 'Black Sox Scandal.' Football: The Green Bay Packers were founded in Wisconsin and have won the most NFL Championship Titles with 13. The Harvard University Crimson (9-0-1) and the University of Illinois Fighting Illini (6-1-0) were national co-champions of college football. Boxing: Jack Dempsey first became World Heavyweight Champion by knocking out Jess Willard in 4 rounds. Horse Racing: Sir Barton became the first winner of the American Triple Crown by winning the Kentucky Derby, the Preakness Stakes, and the Belmont Stakes.

1920

On January 5, the U.S. population was 106,021,537 people. The average yearly income for a U.S. worker was $1,116, equal to $12,185 today; the average house cost $8,094, equal to $88,373 today; the average car cost $575, equal to $6,278 today; a gallon of gas cost 18 cents, equal to $1.96 today; and an electric washing machine cost $85, equal to $928 today.

BIRTHS: Singer Peggy Lee (May 26) supplied the singing and speaking voices for 4 characters in the 1955 Disney film *Lady and the Tramp.* Writer Charles Bukowski (August 16) wrote thousands of poems, hundreds of short stories, and 6 novels, mostly involving the ordinary lives of poor Americans. Timothy Leary (October 22) was a psychologist and writer who advocated the use of psychedelic drugs for their therapeutic benefits. Jazz pianist Dave Brubeck (December 6) is known for using unusual time signatures in his music, evidenced in his most famous piece "Take Five," which is in 5/4 time.

ART: Sculptor Daniel Chester French completed 3 famous projects, 2 in Washington D.C.: the colossal 30-foot tall *Abraham Lincoln* statue that sits in the Lincoln Memorial and the Dupont Circle Fountain; as well as the *Wisconsin* statue on top of the Wisconsin Capitol Building in Madison. Thomas Hart Benton painted the mural *People of Chilmark.*

FILM & RADIO: The top grossing films were *Something to Think About; Way Down East; Over the Hill to the Poorhouse;* and *Pollyanna.* Humphrey Bogart, Greta, Garbo, Claude Rains, and Mary Astor made their film debuts. The first commercial radio station in the U.S., KDKA, began broadcasting on November 20. Announcer Leo Rosenberg said, "This is KDKA of the Westinghouse Electric and Manufacturing Company in East Pittsburgh, Pennsylvania. We shall now broadcast the election returns."

INDUSTRY: New car models included the Hudson Race Car, the Packard Open Roadster, and the Studebaker Six Touring Roadster.

LITERATURE: Works published include F. Scott Fitzgerald's *This Side of Paradise;* Sinclair Lewis' *Main Street;* Edith Wharton's *The Age of Innocence;* Eugene O'Neill's *Beyond the Horizon;* and D.H. Lawrence's *Women in Love.*

MUSIC: Popular songs were Mamie Smith's "Crazy Blues (which became the first vocal blues recording by an African-American artist);" Ben Selvin's "Dardenella;" Al Jolson's "I've Got My Captain Working for Me Now;" John Steel's "Love Nest;" and Paul Whiteman's "Whispering."

SPORTS: Baseball: The AL's Cleveland Indians beat the NL's Brooklyn Dodgers 5 games to 2 in the World Series. The Boston Red Sox sold Babe Ruth to the New York Yankees for $125,000. He hit 54 home runs for the Yankees in 1920, nearly double the record of 29 he had hit for Boston in 1919. Football: The National Football League was founded as the American Professional Association in Canton, Ohio. It started as a coalition of teams from the Ohio League, the New York Pro Football League, the Chicago Football League, and other teams in the Midwestern U.S. The Akron Pros finished with a record of 8-0-3 in the inaugural season to win the first NFL Championship. The only original teams that remain in the NFL today are the Bears, who were founded as the Decatur Staleys and the Cardinals, who started in Chicago. Gaston Chevrolet won the Indy 500, becoming the first driver to complete the race without making a tire change.

1921

BIRTHS: Actress Carol Channing (January 31) won 3 Tony Awards and starred in the original Broadway productions of *Gentlemen Prefer Blondes* in 1949 and *Hello, Dolly!* in 1964. Musical arranger Nelson Riddle (June 1) worked with vocalists Frank Sinatra, Ella Fitzgerald, Nat King Cole, Judy Garland, Dean Martin, Peggy Lee, Johnny Mathis, and Linda Ronstadt, among others. Writer Alex Haley (August 11) based his novel *Roots: The Saga of an American Family* on his own family's history originating in Africa. TV sportscaster Jim McKay (September 24) hosted ABC TV's *Wide World of Sports* from 1961 to 1998 and also covered 12 Olympic Games for ABC.

ARCHITECTURE: The Corn Palace in Mitchell, South Dakota was completed. The outside of the Moorish Revival arena is decorated with crop art murals and hosts the home basketball games of Dakota Wesleyan University Tigers and the Mitchell High School Kernels.

FILM & RADIO: The top grossing films were *The Four Horsemen of the Apocalypse; The Kid; The Three Musketeers; Little Lord Fauntleroy;* and *The Love Light.* The comedy duo of Stan Laurel and Oliver Hardy appeared together for the first time in the film *The Lucky Dog.* Carol Lombard, Basil Rathbone, and Fredric March made their film debuts. Pittsburgh radio station KDKA was home to many radio firsts: April 11, first broadcast of a sporting event: a 10-round, no decision boxing match between Johnny Ray and Johnny Dundee from Pittsburgh's Motor Square Garden. August 5, first play-by-play broadcast of a baseball game: The Pittsburgh Pirates' 8-5 victory over the Philadelphia Phillies at Pittsburgh's Forbes Field. October 8, first play-by-play broadcast of a football game: the University of Pittsburgh Panthers' 21-13 win over the West Virginia University Mountaineers at Forbes Field in Pittsburgh.

INDUSTRY: The Curtiss Candy Company of Chicago, Illinois introduced the Baby Ruth chocolate bar. It was named after President Grover Cleveland's daughter, Ruth, and not the baseball star Babe Ruth. The fast food hamburger chain White Castle was founded in Wichita, Kansas, with their burgers priced at 5 cents.

MUSIC: Popular songs were Richard Whiting's "Ain't We Got Fun?;" Eubie Blake's "I'm Just Wild About Harry;" Marion Harris' "Look for the Silver Lining;" Eddie Cantor's "Margie;" and Isham Jones' "Wabash Blues." Mary Stafford became the first black woman to record for Columbia Records.

SPORTS: Baseball: The NL's New York Giants beat the AL's New York Yankees 5 games to 3 in the World Series. The Yankees' Babe Ruth hit 59 home runs to set a new single season record for the 3rd consecutive year. Football: The Chicago Staleys defeated the Buffalo All-Americans 10-7 to win the NFL Championship. Boxing: Jack Dempsey won the 'Battle of the Century' with a 4th round knockout of Georges Carpentier, before a crowd of over 80,000 in Jersey City, New Jersey. Tennis: The U.S defeated Japan 5-0 to win the Davis Cup at the West Side Tennis Club in New York City. Athletics: Charles Paddock broke the world record in the men's 100-meter dash with a time of 10.4 seconds in Redlands, California.

THEATRE: Eugene O'Neill's play *Anna Christie* won the Pulitzer Prize for drama. *Shuffle Along* was the first successful African-American musical. Theaters opened: The Chicago Theatre, Kansas City's Mainstreet Theater, and the Wilma Theatre in Missoula, Montana.

1922

BIRTHS: Actress Betty White (January 17) has won 7 Emmy Awards from 20 nominations in a career spanning over seventy years on the hit TV shows *The Mary Tyler Moore Show, The Golden Girls,* and *Hot in Cleveland.* Writer Jack Kerouac (March 12) helped pioneer the Beat Generation with works such as *On the Road, Desolation Angels,* and *Big Sur.* Actress Judy Garland (June 10) starred as Dorothy Gale in the 1939 film *The Wizard of Oz* and remains the youngest recipient (at age 39) of the Cecil B. DeMille Award for lifetime achievement in the motion picture industry. Bill Blass (June 22) was a fashion designer whose company grew into a $700 million a year business by 1998.

FILM & RADIO: The top grossing films were *Robin Hood; Oliver Twist; Tess of the Storm Country; Beyond the Rocks;* and *Sherlock Holmes.* The first commercially successful feature length documentary film, *Nanook of the North,* was released. *The Toll of the Sea* was the first film to be produced in Technicolor. Clara Bow, Walt Disney, William Powell, and canine star Rin Tin Tin made their film debuts. Vaudeville star Ed Wynn joined the New York radio station WJZ. His performances became the first radio shows to be broadcast with a live studio audience. Warren G. Harding became the first president to be heard live on radio when he dedicated the Francis Scott Key Memorial in Baltimore, Maryland.

INDUSTRY: Time Inc. was founded in New York City and has grown to publish 130 magazines including *Time, Sports Illustrated, Fortune,* and *People.* Checker Motors Corporation of Kalamazoo, Michigan was known for producing the iconic American taxicab from 1922 to 1982. Pressman Toys was an innovator in licensing games and toys from popular media, such as classic *Little Orphan Annie* and *Dick Tracy* comic strips and *Jeopardy!* and *Wheel of Fortune* game shows. Maidenform brand of women's underwear was the first company to design bras for women of all ages and sizes.

MUSIC: Popular songs were Al Jolson's "April Showers;" Paul Whiteman's "Hot Lips;" Margaret Young's "Way Down Yonder in New Orleans;" George Gershwin's "Do It Again;" and Henry Burr's "My Buddy." Louis Armstrong moved from his native New Orleans to Chicago to join King Oliver's Creole Jazz Band. All musical compositions written in 1922 and before were ruled to be public domain, their intellectual property rights became inapplicable.

SPORTS: The NL's New York Giants swept the AL's New York Yankees 4 games to 0 in the World Series. The Chicago American Giants won their 3rd consecutive Negro League championship. Football: The Canton Bulldogs won the NFL title with a record of 10 wins, 0 losses, and 2 ties. Golf: Gene Sarazen won the U.S. Open at Skokie Country Club in Glencoe, Illinois and the USPGA Championship at Oakmont Country Club in Pennsylvania. Swimming: Johnny Weissmuller broke the 'minute barrier' and created a world record by swimming the 100-meter freestyle in 58.6 seconds. Water sports: Ralph Samuelson invented the sport of water skiing in Lake City, Minnesota.

THEATRE: The play *Abie's Irish Rose* ran for 2,327 performances over 5 years, at the time the longest run in Broadway theater history. George M. Cohan's musical *Little Nellie Kelly* ran for 2 years on Broadway. Theaters opened: Honolulu's Hawaii Theater and Washington D.C.'s Lincoln Theatre.

1923

BIRTHS: Photographer Richard Avedon (May 15) became famous for his portrait photographs of Marilyn Monroe, Dwight David Eisenhower, The Beatles, Andy Warhol, Sly Stone, Nastassja Kinski, and others. Actor James Arness (May 26) is best known for starring as Marshal Matt Dillon in the TV series *Gunsmoke* for 20 years. His younger brother was actor Peter Graves, who starred in the TV series *Mission: Impossible*. World Heavyweight Boxing Champion Rocky Marciano (September 1) is the only heavyweight champion to go undefeated and untied throughout his career, with a record of 49-0. Hank Williams (September 17) was a singer-songwriter who is regarded by many as the greatest country music artist of all time. He recorded 35 singles, 11 of which became number one hit records.

FILM: Popular films were *The Covered Wagon; The Hunchback of Notre Dame; The Ten Commandments; The White Sister;* and *Safety Last!* (featuring the famous scene of actor Harold Lloyd hanging from the hands of a clock high above the street). Lee De Forest demonstrated the Phonofilm synchronized sound system at the Rivoli Theater in New York City. Gary Cooper, Marlene Dietrich, Jean Arthur, and Fay Wray made their film debuts.

INDUSTRY: The largest media conglomerate in the world, The Walt Disney Company, was founded in Los Angeles, California as the Disney Brothers Cartoon Studio. Kenworth, a maker of medium and heavy-duty tractor-trailer trucks, was founded in Kirkland, Washington. America's largest manufacturer of modern office furniture, equipment, and home furnishings, Herman Miller, Inc. was founded in Zeeland, Michigan. The candy bars Butterfinger, Milky Way, and Reese's Peanut Butter Cups were introduced.

LITERATURE: *One of Ours,* by Willa Cather won the Pulitzer Prize for the Novel. A collection of poems by Robert Frost, *New Hampshire,* won the Pulitzer Prize for Poetry. It contained some of Frost's most well-known poems, such as "Stopping by Woods on a Snowy Evening," "Nothing Gold Can Stay," and "Fire and Ice." Ernest Hemingway had his first book published, *Three Stories and Ten Poems.* Edgar Rice Burroughs wrote *Tarzan and the Golden Lion.*

MUSIC: Popular songs were Bessie Smith's "Down Hearted Blues;" Billy Jones' "Yes! We Have No Bananas;" Paul Whiteman's "Parade of the Wooden Soldiers;" Van & Schenck's "(Nothing Could Be Finer Than to be in) Carolina in the Morning;" and Jelly Roll Morton's "King Porter's Stomp." Many African American musicians made their first recordings such as Louis Armstrong, Ida Cox, Bessie Smith, Joe 'King' Oliver, Jelly Roll Morton, and Sidney Bechet.

SPORTS: Baseball: The AL's New York Yankees beat the NL's New York Giants 4 games to 2 in the World Series. The Kansas City Monarchs won their first Negro National League championship. Yankee Stadium opened in the Bronx, New York on April 18. Football: The Canton Bulldogs were the NFL Champions with a record of 11-0-1. Golf: Bobby Jones won the U.S. Open at the Inwood Country Club in New York. Tennis: Bill Tilden defeated Bill Johnston to win the American Men's Singles Final and Helen Wills Moody defeated Molla Bjurstedt Mallory in the American Women's Singles Final at the U.S. National Championships (now known as the U.S. Open) in Philadelphia, Pennsylvania.

1924

BIRTHS: Socialite Gloria Vanderbilt (February 20) launched a line of tight fitting designer jeans with her name embossed on the back pocket in 1976. She is the mother of CNN's Anderson Cooper. Professional basketball player George Mikan (June 18) was a 5-time NBA champion with the Minneapolis Lakers and was selected as one of the 50 Greatest NBA Players of All Time in 1996. Businessman Lee Iacocca (October 15) engineered the Ford Mustang before reviving the Chrysler Corporation as CEO in the 1980s with his trademark TV commercial phrase, 'If you can find a better car, buy it.' Rod Serling (December 25) wrote the award-winning 1956 teleplay *Requiem for a Heavyweight* and created the TV series *The Twilight Zone* in 1959.

FILM & RADIO: The top films were *The Marriage Circle; The Sea Hawk; He Who Gets Slapped; Girl Shy;* and *A Society Scandal.* Entertainment entrepreneur Marcus Loew created Metro-Goldwyn-Mayer film studios by gaining control of Metro Pictures, Goldwyn Pictures Corporation, and Louis B. Mayer Pictures. Famous silent film director Thomas 'The Father of the Western' Ince died of a reported hear attack in his bed in Los Angeles on November 19. Rumors soon surfaced that he was shot dead by publishing tycoon William Randolph Hearst in a jealous rage. Clark Gable and John Gielgud made their film debuts. Calvin Coolidge made the first presidential political speech on radio from New York City on February 12 to an audience of 5 million listeners. Still on the air today, KFOR in Lincoln, Nebraska began broadcasting on March 4. Jack Buck, the radio announcer for Major League baseball's St. Louis Cardinals from 1954 to 2000, was born on August 21.

INDUSTRY: The Computing Tabulating Recording Company changed its name to International Business Machines on February 14. Today, IBM is the second largest U.S. company with 433,362 employees. Alice Vanderbilt Morris founded the International Auxiliary Language Association, later known as Interlingua. The first Macy's Thanksgiving Day Parade was held in New York City on November 27.

MUSIC: Popular songs were Al Jolson's "California, Here I Come;" Isham Jones' "I'll See You in My Dreams;" Gus Kahn's "It Had To Be You;" Vincent Youmans' "Tea For Two;" and Ma Rainey's "See See Rider." One of the most popular of all American concert works, George Gershwin's "Rhapsody in Blue," was first performed on February 12 at Aeolian Hall in New York City by Paul Whiteman's Orchestra, with Gershwin playing piano.

SPORTS: Baseball: The AL's Washington Senators defeated the NL's New York Giants 4 games to 3 in the World Series. Football: The Cleveland Bulldogs were NFL Champions with a record of 7-1-1. The Knute Rockne coached University of Notre Dame Fighting Irish were college football champions, led by the 'Four Horsemen' to an undefeated record of 10-0. The first Winter Olympics were held in Chamonix, France. Norway won the most medals (18) and the most gold medals (5). The U.S. won the most medals (99) and the most gold medals (45) at the Summer Olympics in Rome.

THEATRE: Hatcher Hughes' play *Hell-Bent Fer Heaven* won the Pulitzer Prize for Drama. Eugene O'Neill's play *Desire Under the Elms* was published. The musical *I'll Say She Is* starred the Marx Brothers and helped launch them into Broadway theatre stardom, and later into films.

1925

BIRTHS: Yogi Berra (May 12) was an 18-time All-Star, 13-time World Series champion, and 3-time American League MVP during his 19-year career as catcher for the New York Yankees. B.B. King (September 16) is ranked number 6 on *Rolling Stone* magazine's list of the 100 greatest guitarists of all time. Writer Elmore Leonard (October 11) has written many novels and short stories that have been adapted into movies including *3:10 to Yuma, Hombre, Mr. Majestyk, Get Shorty, 52 Pick-Up,* and *Jackie Brown.* Stand-up comic Lenny Bruce (October 13) was renowned for his critical, free-style form of comedy. His trial for obscenity, in which he was eventually found not guilty, is seen as a landmark decision for freedom of speech.

FILM: The top films were *The Big Parade; Ben-Hur* (which was the most expensive silent movie ever made at a cost of $5 million); *His People; Little Annie Rooney;* and *The Unholy Three.* Gary Cooper, Joan Crawford, Tyrone Power, and Myrna Loy made their film debuts.

INDUSTRY: Walter Chrysler founded the automobile manufacturer Chrysler Corporation in Detroit, Michigan on June 6. Charles Francis Jenkins sent the first synchronized transmission of pictures and sound over a distance of 5 miles. Jenkins called this earliest form of television, 'the first public demonstration of 'radiovision.' Arthur Heineman created the first motel in the world, the Milestone Mo-Tel, in San Luis Obispo, California. It cost $80,000 to build and originally charged $1.25 per room per night.

LITERATURE: Works published include: F. Scott Fitzgerald's *The Great Gatsby,* later named by the Modern Library as the second best novel of the 20th Century; Ernest Hemingway's first collection of short stories, *In Our Time;* and Sinclair Lewis' *Arrowsmith.*

MUSIC: Popular songs were Ben Bernie's "Sweet Georgia Brown;" Eddie Cantor's "If You Knew Susie;" Bessie Smith's "St. Louis Blues;" Ace Brigode's "Yes Sir, That's My Baby;" and Richard Rogers' "Here in My Arms." Blind Lemon Jefferson and Lonnie Johnson made their recording debuts. One of the most important advances in recording history occurred when Victor, Columbia, and HMV phonograph companies switched from traditional acoustic recording methods to new electric microphone technology.

SPORTS: Baseball: The NL's Pittsburgh Pirates defeated the AL's Washington Senators 4 games to 3 in the World Series. The Pirates were the first team to come back and win a World Series after being down 3 games to 1. Football: The Chicago Cardinals were NFL Champions as 5 new teams joined the league: the New York Giants, the Detroit Panthers, the Canton Bulldogs, the Providence Steam Roller, and the Pottsville Maroons. The University of Alabama Crimson Tide were college football champions, with their first ever undefeated season at 10-0. The American Basketball League was founded as the first major league of professional basketball. The Cleveland Rosenblums swept the Brooklyn Arcadians 3 games to 0 to win the first ABL Title.

THEATRE: The play *Hell's Bells* opened on Broadway starring Humphrey Bogart and Shirley Booth. The Marx Brothers musical *The Cocoanuts* opened at Broadway's Lyric Theatre on December 8. When the Uptown Theatre opened in Chicago, it was the largest theatre in the U.S., with 4,281 seats.

1926

BIRTHS: Hugh Hefner (April 9) created *Playboy* magazine in 1953. The first issue featured nude photographs of actress Marilyn Monroe and sold over 50,000 copies. Author Harper Lee (April 28) wrote the 1960 Pulitzer Prize winning novel *To Kill a Mockingbird,* which has sold over 30 million copies and has been translated into 40 languages. Jazz trumpeter Miles Davis (May 26) was one of the most influential musicians of the 20th century. His 1959 album *Kind of Blue* is the best selling jazz record of all time with sales of over 4 million copies. Marilyn Monroe (June 1), born Norma Jean Mortenson, was ranked as the 6th greatest female star of all time by the American Film Institute and is regarded as the quintessential American sex symbol.

ARCHITECTURE: The 10-story, 184-foot tall Aloha Tower lighthouse at Pier 9 of Honolulu Harbor opened in Hawaii.

FILM: The top films were *Aloma of the South Seas; Flesh and the Devil; Sparrows; The Temptress;* and *The Sea Beast.* The Vitaphone system of synchronizing background audio with film debuted with the film *Don Juan.* John Wayne and Janet Gaynor made their film debuts.

INDUSTRY: The first major broadcast network in the U.S., the National Broadcasting Corporation (NBC) was founded in New York City with 2 radio stations: WEAF and WJZ. U.S. Route 66, the iconic highway that ran 2,448 miles from Chicago to Los Angeles, was established on November 11. United Airlines started as Varney Air Lines air mail service in Boise, Idaho. The Maid-Rite 'loose meat' sandwich restaurant chain was founded in Des Moines, Iowa.

LITERATURE: Ernest Hemingway's greatest work, the novel *The Sun Also Rises,* was published. The book details a group of American and British expatriates who travel from Paris, France to the Festival of San Fermin in Pamplona, Spain to watch bullfights and the running of the bulls.

MUSIC: Popular songs were Duke Ellington's "East St. Louis Toodle-Oo;" George and Ira Gershwin's "Someone to Watch Over Me;" Gene Austin's "Bye Bye Blackbird;" Al Jolson's "I'm Sitting on Top of the World;" and Irving Kaufman's "Tonight You Belong to Me." Bing Crosby made his first recording, "I've Got the Girl."

SPORTS: Baseball: The NL's St. Louis Cardinals defeated the AL's New York Yankees 4 games to 3 in the World Series. Mule Suttles of the St. Louis Stars set Negro League records with 27 home runs, 21 triples, and a .498 batting average. Football: The Frankford Yellow Jackets of Philadelphia were NFL Champions with a 14-1-1 record. Golf: Bobby Jones became the first golfer to win the British Open and U.S. Open titles in the same year. Horse Racing: Bubbling Over won the Kentucky Derby.

THEATRE: Actress Barbara Stanwyck made her acting debut in the play *The Noose* on October 20 at Broadway's Hudson Theatre. Mae West wrote and starred in the play *Sex*, for which she was charged with obscenity and fined $500. The resulting publicity increased her fame. The Richard Rodgers and Lorenz Hart musical *The Girl Friend* opened on Broadway's Vanderbilt Theatre March 17. Theaters opened: Chicago's Congress Theater; San Francisco's Harding Theater; and Los Angeles' Westlake Theatre.

1927

BIRTHS: Bob Fosse (June 23) won a record 8 Tony Awards for choreography and the 1972 Best Director Academy Award for the musical film *Cabaret* (beating Francis Ford Coppola for *The Godfather*). Playwright Neil Simon (July 4) has received more Oscar and Tony award nominations than any other writer, for such works as *Barefoot in the Park* in 1963 and *The Odd Couple* in 1965. Professional tennis player Althea Gibson (August 25) became the first African-American woman to win a Grand Slam title when she won the French Open in 1956. Geoffrey Beene (August 30) won 8 Coty Fashion Awards during his 40-plus year career as a leading fashion designer.

ART & ARCHITECTURE: Edward Hopper's realist painting *Automat* was sold for $1,200 after being displayed at the Rehn Galleries in New York City. Today the painting is owned by the Des Moines Art Center in Iowa. When the Art Deco style 47-story, 555-foot tall LeVeque Tower opened in Columbus, Ohio, it was the 5th tallest building in the world.

FILM & RADIO: Al Jolson's *The Jazz Singer* was the first feature-length film to use synchronized dialogue sequences. As the 'talkies' signaled the end of the silent film era, it became Warner Bros. highest grossing film to date, earning $4 million. Other top films were *Love; Metropolis; Jesse James;* and *My Best Girl.* Douglas Fairbanks established the Academy of Motion Picture Arts and Sciences in Los Angeles with the film *Wings* winning the first Best Picture Academy Award. NBC made the first nationwide radio broadcast of college football's Rose Bowl game on January 1.

INDUSTRY: The convenience store chain 7-Eleven, named for its original store hours of 7am to 11pm, was founded in Dallas, Texas. Pan Am Airways was founded and began passenger service from Key West, Florida to Havana, Cuba. The Ford motor company introduced the Model A as its new automobile after 19 years of Model T production. Prices ranged from $385 for a roadster to $1,400 for a top of the line 'Town Car.'

LITERATURE: Thornton Wilder's second novel, *The Bridge of San Luis Rey,* won the Pulitzer Prize for the Novel.

MUSIC: Popular songs were Hoagy Carmichael's "Stardust;" Jerome Kern's "Ol' Man River;" Harry Woods' "Side By Side;" Irving Berlin's "Blue Skies;" and Al Jolson's "Me and My Shadow."

SPORTS: The AL's New York Yankees, led by their strong group of hitters nicknamed Murderers' Row, swept the NL's Pittsburgh Pirates 4 games to 0 in the World Series. The Yankees' Babe Ruth hit a major league record 60 home runs in 1927. Football: The New York Giants were NFL Champions with a record of 11-1-1. Boxing: Gene Tunney retained his World Heavyweight Championship by defeating Jack Dempsey in 10 rounds at Soldier Field in Chicago in 'The Battle of the Long Count.' Tunney was knocked down for 13 seconds in the 7th round but the count was delayed because Dempsey did not retire to a neutral corner.

THEATRE: Regarded as the first truly great American musical, *Show Boat* ran on Broadway for a year and a half and a total of 572 shows. The Broadway version of the play *Dracula* starred Bela Lugosi in his first major English-speaking role. Fred Astaire and his sister Adele starred in the Ira and George Gershwin musical *Funny Face.*

1928

BIRTHS: Fred Rogers (March 20) won 4 Emmy Awards for creating and hosting the children's TV show *Mister Rogers' Neighborhood,* which ran from 1968 to 2001. Child star Shirley Temple (April 23) was Hollywood's top box office draw from 1935 to 1938, starting her film career at the age of 3 and retiring completely from films at the age of 22. Composer Burt Bacharach (May 12) has written 70 top 40 hit songs including "Raindrops Keep Falling on my Head," which won the 1969 Academy Award for Best Original Song from the film *Butch Cassidy and the Sundance Kid.* Artist Andy Warhol (August 6) led the visual art movement known as Pop Art with his paintings of Campbell's soup cans, Coca-Cola bottles, and Marilyn Monroe.

FILM & RADIO: Popular films were *The Road to Ruin; A Woman of Affairs; Noah's Ark; Our Dancing Daughters;* and the first all-talking feature film, *Lights of New York.* Cartoon characters Mickey and Minnie Mouse made their debuts in the Walt Disney animated short film, *Steamboat Willie.* It was the first film to include a soundtrack completely created in post-production, including sound effects, music, and dialogue. Others making their film debuts included Humphrey Bogart, Jean Harlow, Charles Laughton, and Randolph Scott. One of the first radio comedy series, *Amos 'n' Andy,* premiered on WMAQ in Chicago and ran nightly until 1943.

INDUSTRY: To help customers pronounce his name correctly, Italian immigrant Ettore Boiardi changed the spelling and started the Chef Boyardee canned pasta company in Cleveland, Ohio. The Plymouth car company was founded in Detroit, Michigan. The Sports Authority sporting goods retail chain started in Denver, Colorado. Dreyer's Ice Cream Company was founded in Oakland, California.

MUSIC: Popular songs were Harry Ruby's "I Wanna Be Loved by You;" Kurt Weill's "Mack The Knife;" Louis Armstrong's "West End Blues;" Walter Donaldson's "Makin' Whoopee;" and Blind Willie McTell's "Statesboro Blues." Leroy Carr, whose style later influenced Nat King Cole and Ray Charles, released his first, and most famous song, "How Long, How Long Blues."

SPORTS: Baseball: The AL's New York Yankees swept the NL's St. Louis Cardinals 4 games to 0 to win the World Series. Football: The Providence Steam Roller were NFL Champions with an 8-1-2 record. The Georgia Institute of Technology Yellow Jackets with a 10-0 record and the University of Southern California Trojans with a 9-0-1 record were college football co-national champions. Basketball: The New York Celtics (an early professional barnstorming team with no relation to the modern Boston Celtics) defeated the Fort Wayne Hoosiers 3 games to 1 to win the ABL Championship. Hockey: The New York Rangers defeated the Montreal Maroons 3 games to 2 to win the Stanley Cup. Boxing: World Heavyweight Champion Gene Tunney retired after defeating Tom Heeney with a 12th round technical knockout in the Bronx, New York. Golf: Johnny Farrell won the U.S. Open Championship at Olympia Fields Country Club in Chicago, Illinois. Bobby Jones won the U.S. Amateur Championship at the Brae Burn Country Club in Newton, Massachusetts.

THEATRE: Eugene O'Neill's play *Strange Interlude* won the Pulitzer Prize for Drama. At more than 4 hours, the play was sometimes performed with a dinner break, or over consecutive evenings.

1929

BIRTHS: Liz Claiborne (March 31) created the fashion company Liz Claiborne Inc., which in 1986 became the first company founded by a woman to make the Fortune 500 list. Arnold Palmer (September 10) was golf's first TV superstar by winning 95 professional golf tournaments worldwide including 7 major championships. Berry Gordy, Jr. (November 28) founded Motown Records in Detroit, Michigan in 1959 and helped launch the careers of Stevie Wonder, Michael Jackson, Smokey Robinson, and The Supremes. Dick Clark (November 30) hosted American television's longest running variety show, *American Bandstand,* from 1957 to 1987.

ART & ARCHITECTURE: The Museum of Modern Art opened in New York City to 47,000 visitors on November 7 for an exhibition of works by Gauguin, Cezanne, Seurat, and van Gogh. Edward Hopper created the oil on canvas painting, *Chop Suey*. Architect Richard Neutra designed and built the first steel frame house in the U.S., the Lovell House in Los Angeles, California. The San Francisco Bay Toll-Bridge opened on March 2 as the longest bridge in the world.

FILM: The first Academy Awards ceremony was held at the Hollywood Roosevelt Hotel in Los Angeles, California, hosted by Douglas Fairbanks. Tickets cost 5 dollars, 270 people attended, and the ceremony lasted 15 minutes. The 1927 silent film, *Wings,* starring Clara Bow and Gary Cooper, won the first Best Picture Academy Award. Popular films of 1928 were *The Broadway Melody* (the first major musical film of the sound era)*; Welcome Danger; The Desert Song; Bulldog Drummond;* and *Coquette*. The Walt Disney Pictures film studio was founded in Burbank, California. Judy Garland, Betty Grable, Johnny Weissmuller, Ray Milland, and Paul Muni made their film debuts.

INDUSTRY: Farmland Foods rose to become the largest U.S. agricultural cooperative, owned by more than 600,000 farm families. Macy's department store chain was founded in Columbus, Ohio. The western footwear manufacturer, Acme Boots, was founded in Chicago, Illinois. Hawaiian Airlines started as Inter-Island Airways and has never had a fatal accident, the oldest U.S. carrier with that distinction.

MUSIC: Popular songs were Helen Kane's "Button Up Your Overcoat;" Cliff Edwards' "Singin' in the Rain;" Nick Lucas' "Tip Toe Thru The Tulips;" Irving Berlin's "Puttin' on the Ritz;" and Cole Porter's "You Do Something To Me."

SPORTS: Baseball: The AL's Philadelphia Athletics defeated the NL's Chicago Cubs 4 games to 1 in the World Series. Football: The Green Bay Packers were NFL Champions with a 12-0-1 record. The University of Notre Dame Fighting Irish were college football national champions with a 9-0 record. Basketball: The Cleveland Rosenblums swept the Fort Wayne Hoosiers 4 games to 0 to win the ABL Championship. Hockey: The Boston Bruins defeated the New York Rangers 2 games to 0 to win the Stanley Cup. Golf: Bobby Jones won the U.S. Open Championship at Winged Foot Golf Club in Mamaroneck, New York. Motor Racing: Ray Keech won the Indianapolis 500 auto race in Indianapolis, Indiana.

THEATRE: Elmer Rice's play, *Street Scene,* won the Pulitzer Prize for Drama.

1930

On April 1, the U.S. population was 122,775,046 people. The average yearly income for a U.S. worker was $1,170, equal to $15,329 today; the average house cost $7,543, equal to $98,828 today; the average car cost $480, equal to $6,289 today; a gallon of gas cost 17 cents, equal to $2.22 today; and a dozen eggs cost 18 cents, equal to $2.35 today.

BIRTHS: Pop Artist Jasper Johns (May 15) uses flags, maps, targets, stenciled words and numbers as themes in his paintings and print works. Actor Clint Eastwood (May 31) has been nominated for 10 Academy Awards, winning 4, including Best Director for the 1992 film *Unforgiven* and 2003's *Million Dollar Baby.* Astronaut Neil Armstrong (August 5) was the first person to set foot upon the Moon on July 20, 1969, saying "That's one small step for a man, one giant leap for mankind." Musician Ray Charles (September 23) pioneered the genre of soul music by fusing rhythm and blues, gospel, and blues styles into his early recordings in the 1950s.

ART & ARCHITECTURE: Grant Wood painted *American Gothic,* one of the most famous paintings in the history of American art. Sculptor Malvina Hoffman created 105 bronze statues representing humans from diverse cultures for the permanent exhibit, Hall of Man, at Chicago's Field Museum. New York City's Chrysler Building became the world's first man-made structure taller than 1,000 feet (1,046). The Chicago Board of Trade Building held the title of tallest building in Chicago until 1965.

FILM & RADIO: *All Quiet on the Western Front* won the Best Picture Academy Award. Other top films were *Tom Sawyer; Ingagi; Feet First; Anna Christie;* and *Romance.* James Cagney, Spencer Tracy, Ginger Rogers, Irene Dunn, Peter Lorre, and cartoon character Betty Boop made their film debuts.

The crime-fighting vigilante *The Shadow* debuted as a radio drama on July 31 with the famous introduction: "Who knows what evil lurks in the hearts of men? The Shadow knows!"

INDUSTRY: Baker James Alexander invented the Hostess brand snack cake Twinkie, which was originally filled with banana cream, but switched to vanilla cream when bananas were rationed during World War II. Clarence Birdseye created retail frozen foods in Springfield, Massachusetts. The 3M Company introduced Scotch Tape on September 8 in Saint Paul, Minnesota.

LITERATURE: Works published include Dashiell Hammett's *The Maltese Falcon;* William Faulkner's *As I Lay Dying;* Pearl S. Buck's *East Wind: West Wind;* Langston Hughes' *Not Without Laughter;* and Philip Gordon Wylie's *Gladiator.* Sinclair Lewis was awarded the Nobel Prize in Literature.

MUSIC: Popular songs were George and Ira Gershwin's "Embraceable You;" Hoagy Carmichael's "Georgia On My Mind;" Cole Porter's "Love For Sale;" Eubie Blake's "Memories of You;" and Johnny Green's "Body and Soul."

SPORTS: Baseball: The AL's Philadelphia Athletics defeated the NL's St. Louis Cardinals 4 games to 2 in the World Series. Football: The Green Bay Packers won the NFL Title with a record of 10-3-1. The University of Alabama Crimson Tide (10-0) and the University of Notre Dame Fighting Irish (10-0) were college football co-national champions. Golf: Bobby Jones became the only player to win golfing's Grand Slam: Champion of the British Open, U.S. Open, British Amateur, and U.S. Amateur, all in the same year. Motor Racing: Billy Arnold won the Indianapolis 500 at an average speed of 100.448 miles per hour, the first time a winner averaged over 100 mph.

1931

BIRTHS: Concert promoter Bill Graham (January 8) operated the Fillmore West and Winterland concert venues in San Francisco, as well as the Fillmore East in New York City. James Dean (February 8) starred in only 3 movies: *East of Eden, Rebel Without a Cause,* and *Giant,* yet he remains an American cultural icon whose image still earns his estate $5 million per year. Major League Baseball star Willie Mays (May 6) was a 24-time All Star and a 12-time Gold Glove Award winner. He placed second on *The Sporting News* magazine's list of the 100 Greatest Baseball Players (behind Babe Ruth). Conceptual artist John Baldessari (June 17) has created thousands of works in film, printmaking, installation, sculpture, painting, and photography.

ART & ARCHITECTURE: Georgia O'Keeffe produced the oil on canvas painting *Cow's Skull: Red, White, and Blue.* Cartoonist Chester Gould created the *Dick Tracy* comic strip, which debuted on October 4 in the *Detroit Mirror* newspaper. Gould wrote and drew the strip until 1977. At 102 stories and 1,454 feet tall, New York City's Empire State Building stood as the world's tallest building for 40 years. The George Washington Bridge spans the Hudson River, connecting Manhattan in New York City to Fort Lee, New Jersey and is the world's busiest motor vehicle bridge, carrying 106 million vehicles per year.

FILM & RADIO: *Cimarron* won the Best Picture Academy Award. Other top films were *Frankenstein* starring Boris Karloff; *Mata Hari* starring Greta Garbo; *Kiki* starring Mary Pickford; and *City Lights* starring Charlie Chaplin. Bette Davis, Bruce Cabot, and Otto Preminger made their film debuts. Bing Crosby's weekly CBS Radio program ran from 1931 to 1962.

INDUSTRY: New York chemist Lawrence Gelb and his wife Joan Clair founded the Clairol personal care company after seeing the popularity of hair-coloring products while traveling in France.

LITERATURE: Elizabeth Coatsworth's children's novel *The Cat Who Went to Heaven* won the Newbery Medal.

MUSIC: Popular songs were Herman Hupfeld's "As Time Goes By;" Cab Calloway's "Minnie the Moocher;" Gus Kahn's "Dream a Little Dream of Me;" Ray Noble's "Goodnight, Sweetheart;" and Louis Armstrong's "Lazy River." The *Star-Spangled Banner* was officially named the U.S. national anthem.

SPORTS: Baseball: The NL's St. Louis Cardinals defeated the AL's Philadelphia Athletics 4 games to 3 in the World Series. The first modern MVP awards were given to 2nd baseman Frankie Frisch of the NL's St. Louis Cardinals and pitcher Lefty Grove of the AL's Boston Red Sox. The Negro League played its final season with the St. Louis Stars winning the last championship. Football: The Green Bay Packers were NFL Champions with a 13-2 record. The University of Southern California Trojans were college football national champions with a 10-1 record. Basketball: The Brooklyn Visitations defeated the Fort Wayne Hoosiers 4 games to 2 to win the ABL Championship. The first Associated Press (AP) Male and Female Athlete of the Year Awards went to Pepper Martin in baseball and Helene Madison in swimming.

THEATRE: Eugene O'Neill's play *Mourning Becomes Electra* premiered at Broadway's Guild Theatre on October 26 and ran for 150 performances.

1932

BIRTHS: John Williams (February 8) has composed some of the most famous film scores in Hollywood history including *Jaws, Star Wars, E.T. the Extra Terrestrial,* and *Indiana Jones.* Actress Elizabeth Taylor (February 27) won 2 Best Actress Academy Awards for the films *Butterfield 8* in 1960 and *Who's Afraid of Virginia Woolf?* in 1966. Halston (April 23) was a fashion designer whose styles fit the international jet set and discotheque crowds of the 1970s. Dave Thomas (July 2) founded the fast food hamburger chain Wendy's (named after his daughter) and appeared in over 800 commercials from 1989 to 2002, more than any other company founder in TV history.

FILM & RADIO: *Grand Hotel* starring Greta Garbo won the Best Picture Academy Award. Other top films were *Shanghai Express* starring Marlene Dietrich; *Dr. Jekyll and Mr. Hyde* starring Fredric March; *Emma* starring Marie Dressler; *Movie Crazy* starring Harold Lloyd; and *Red Dust* starring Clark Gable. Walt Disney produced the cartoon *Flowers and Trees,* the first film to use the full 3 strip Technicolor process. Cary Grant, Mae West, Alan Ladd, Katherine Hepburn, and Shirley Temple made their film debuts. On February 15, George Burns and Gracie Allen became regulars on CBS Radio's *The Guy Lombardo Show. The Jack Benny Program* premiered on NBC Radio's Blue Network on May 2.

INDUSTRY: Zippo Lighters were founded in Bradford, Pennsylvania. The Revlon cosmetics company started by developing a new type of nail enamel. Coleco toys took its name from the **Co**nnecticut **Le**ather **Co**mpany. Elmer Doolin paid $100 ($1,580 today) for a corn chip recipe that he turned into Fritos. Playtex, maker of women's undergarments, got its name from 'Perforated Latex.' Golf equipment manufacturer Titleist was founded in Fairhaven, Massachusetts.

LITERATURE: Pearl S. Buck's *The Good Earth* won the Pulitzer Prize for the Novel and was the best-selling novel in the U.S. in 1931 and 1932.

MUSIC: Popular songs included Fred Astaire's "Night & Day;" Cab Calloway's "I've Got the World on a String;" Duke Ellington's "It Don't Mean a Thing (If It Ain't Got That Swing);" Louie Armstrong's "All of Me;" and Rudy Vallee's "Brother, Can You Spare a Dime?"

SPORTS: Baseball: The AL's New York Yankees swept the NL's Chicago Cubs 4 games to 0 to win the World Series. The Yankees' Babe Ruth hit his famous 'called shot' home run in game 3. Football: The Chicago Bears beat the Portsmouth Spartans 9-0 in the first ever NFL playoff game to become NFL Champions. Due to extremely cold weather, the game was played indoors at the Chicago Stadium on December 18. The University of Southern California Trojans were college football national champions with a record of 10-0. The Winter Olympics were held in Lake Placid, New York with the U.S. team winning the most medals (12) and the most gold medals (6). The Summer Olympics were held in Los Angeles, California with the U.S. team winning the most medals (103) and the most gold medals (41).

THEATRE: Radio City Music Hall in midtown Manhattan, New York City, opened to the public on December 27.

1933

BIRTHS: Music producer Quincy Jones (March 14) has won 27 Grammy Awards from a record 79 nominations. He produced Michael Jackson's 1982 *Thriller* album, which has sold over 110 million copies worldwide. Carol Burnett (April 26) hosted the TV variety program *The Carol Burnett Show* from 1967 to 1978 and has won 6 Emmy Awards. Willie Nelson (April 30) has written some of country music's most popular songs including "Crazy," "Hello Walls," "Pretty Paper," and "Funny How Time Slips Away." Larry King (November 19) hosted the nightly interview TV show *Larry King Live* on CNN from 1985 to 2010, for which he won 2 Peabody Awards and 10 Cable ACE Awards for best interviewer and best talk show series.

ART: Black Mountain College was founded in Black Mountain, North Carolina with an emphasis on art education, attracting notable lecturers including John Cage, Willem de Kooning, and Franz Kline.

FILM & RADIO: *Cavalcade* won the Best Picture Academy Award. Other top films were *I'm No Angel* starring Mae West; *Dinner at Eight* starring John Barrymore and Jean Harlow; *Little Women* starring Katherine Hepburn; *42ⁿᵈ Street* starring Dick Powell, Ruby Keeler, and Ginger Rogers; and *King Kong* starring Fay Wray and Bruce Cabot. Errol Flynn, Dorothy Lamour, Fred Astaire, and Lucille Ball made their film debuts. *The Lone Ranger* radio program premiered on Detroit radio station WXYZ and ran until 1955.

INDUSTRY: Brothers Ernest and Julio Gallo founded the largest exporter of California wines, E & J Gallo Winery, in Modesto, California. Rubbermaid, makers of household items such as food storage containers and trash cans, was founded in Wooster, Ohio. James Ryder started the Ryder rental truck company in Miami, Florida with one truck: a 1931 Ford Model 'A'. The first issue of *Newsweek* magazine was published on February 17, featuring a cover with 7 photographs from the week's news.

LITERATURE: Erle Stanley Gardner's novel *The Case of the Velvet Claws* introduced the character of Defense Attorney Perry Mason. Other published works include *Tarzan and the City of Gold* by Edgar Rice Burroughs; *God's Little Acre* by Erskine Caldwell; and *The Thin Man* by Dashiell Hammett.

MUSIC: Popular songs included Duke Ellington's "Sophisticated Lady;" Dick Powell's "We're In The Money;" Ethel Waters' "Stormy Weather;" Jerome Kern's "Smoke Gets in Your Eyes;" and Bing Crosby's "You're Getting to Be a Habit With Me."

SPORTS: Baseball: The NL's New York Giants defeated the AL's Washington Senators 4 games to 1 in the World Series. Football: The Chicago Bears beat the New York Giants 23-21 to win the NFL Championship. The University of Michigan Wolverines were college football national champions with a 7-0-1 record. Hockey: The New York Rangers won their second Stanley Cup by defeating the Toronto Maple Leafs 3 games to 1 in a best of five series. New York Giants pitcher Carl Hubbell was named the Associated Press' Male Athlete of the Year and tennis player Helen Jacobs won the Female Athlete of the Year award.

THEATRE: The Broadway play *Tobacco Road,* based on the novel by Erskine Caldwell, ran for a total of 3,182 performances, becoming the longest-running play in Broadway history at the time.

1934

BIRTHS: Bill Russell (February 12) played center for the National Basketball Association's Boston Celtics, who won 11 league championships during his 13-year career. Russell also won the NBA Most Valuable Player Award 5 times. Actress Shirley Jones (March 31) starred in the musical films *Oklahoma!, Carousel,* and *The Music Man,* as well as TV's *The Partridge Family.* Michael Graves (July 9) is a postmodernist architect who designed the Indianapolis Art Center and restored the Washington Monument. He has also created a line of household goods for the retail store Target. Charles Manson (November 12) led the criminal cult group known as the Manson Family that murdered actress Sharon Tate and others in 1969 in California.

FILM: *It Happened One Night* became the first film to win all 5 of the major Academy Awards: Best Picture, Best Director for Frank Capra, Best Actor for Clark Gable, Best Actress for Claudette Colbert, and Best Screenplay for Robert Riskin. Other top films were *Viva Villa!* Starring Wallace Beery; *Cleopatra* starring Claudette Colbert; *The Thin Man* starring William Powell and Myrna Loy; *The Gay Divorcee* starring Fred Astaire and Ginger Rogers; *The Girl From Missouri* starring Jean Harlow; and *Babes in Toyland* starring Stan Laurel and Oliver Hardy. Shirley Temple received the first Academy Award given to a child for her performance in *Bright Eyes*, which featured her signature song, "On the Good Ship Lollipop." Gene Autry, Bob Hope, Rosalind Russell, and Robert Taylor made their film debuts.

INDUSTRY: American Airlines was founded in Fort Worth, Texas. Muzak Holdings, the company that supplies background music to elevators, retail stores and other companies, started in Fort Mill, South Carolina. Snack food maker Old Dutch Foods was founded in St. Paul, Minnesota.

LITERATURE: The science fiction comic strip *Flash Gordon* was first published January 7. Other works published include F. Scott Fitzgerald's *Tender Is the Night;* James M. Cain's *The Postman Always Rings Twice;* Henry Miller's *Tropic of Cancer;* and Irving Stone's *Lust for Life.*

MUSIC: Popular songs included Benny Goodman's "Moon Glow;" Bing Crosby's "Love in Bloom;" Fats Waller's "Honeysuckle Rose;" Ray Noble's "The Very Thought Of You;" Guy Lombardo's "Winter Wonderland;" Hoagy Carmichael's "Lazy River;" Harry Warren's "I Only Have Eyes For You;" and Bob Nolan's "Tumbling Tumbleweeds." 17-year-old Ella Fitzgerald made her singing debut at Harlem's Apollo Theater on Amateur Night, November 21. She sang Hoagy Carmichael's "Judy" and won the first prize of $25.

SPORTS: Baseball: The NL's St. Louis Cardinals defeated the AL's Detroit Tigers 4 games to 3 in the World Series. In the 2nd MLB All-Star game, New York Giants pitcher Carl Hubbell struck out Babe Ruth, Lou Gehrig, Jimmie Foxx, Al Simmons, and Joe Cronin consecutively July 10 at New York City's Polo Grounds. Football: The New York Giants beat the Chicago Bears 30-13 in the NFL Championship game. The University of Minnesota Golden Gophers were college football national champions with an 8-0 record. Hockey: The Chicago Black Hawks defeated the Detroit Red Wings 3 games to 1 in a best of 5 series to win the Stanley Cup.

THEATRE: Cole Porter's musical *Anything Goes* opened on Broadway and introduced such songs as "Anything Goes," "I Get a Kick Out of You," and "You're the Top."

1935

BIRTHS: Elvis Presley (January 8) is the best-selling solo artist in the history of popular music with 36 number one singles and 20 number one albums. He is a member of 12 different Halls of Fame including Rock and Roll, Country, Rockabilly, and Gospel. Former Major League Baseball catcher Bob Uecker (January 26) has been the play-by-play radio announcer for the Milwaukee Brewers since 1971. Author Ken Kesey (September 17) wrote the novel *One Flew Over the Cuckoo's Nest* and was a link between the Beat Generation of the 1950s and the 1960s Hippies. Comedian Woody Allen (December 1) has been nominated for 23 Academy Awards, winning Best Director and Best Original Screenplay for his 1978 film *Annie Hall*.

ARCHITECTURE: Designed by architect Cass Gilbert, the United States Supreme Court Building opened in Washington, D.C. Bordering Nevada and Arizona on the Colorado River, the Hoover Dam was dedicated on September 30. More than 100 workers died during its 5-year construction.

FILM: *Mutiny on the Bounty* starring Clark Gable and Charles Laughton won the Best Picture Academy Award. Other top films were *Top Hat* starring Fred Astaire and Ginger Rogers; *Becky Sharp* starring Miriam Hopkins; *The Littlest Rebel* starring Shirley Temple; *China Seas* starring Clark Gable and Jean Harlow; and *Captain Blood* starring Errol Flynn and Olivia de Havilland. Henry Fonda, Ingrid Bergman, Jimmy Stewart, Rita Hayworth, Don Ameche, Joan Fontaine, Roy Rogers, and Danny Kaye made their film debuts.

LITERATURE: The children's novel *Little House on the Prairie* by Laura Ingalls Wilder was published. Other published works include Pearl S. Buck's *A House Divided;* John Steinbeck's *Tortilla Flat;* John Dickson Carr's *The Hollow Man;* and Stanley G. Weinbaum's *The Lotus Eaters.*

MUSIC: Popular songs included Irving Berlin's "Cheek to Cheek;" Cole Porter's "Begin the Beguine;" Guy Lombardo's "Red Sails In the Sunset;" Shirley Temple's "On The Good Ship Lollipop;" Nelson Eddy's "When I Grow Too Old To Dream;" The Dorsey Brothers' "Lullaby of Broadway;" and Fats Waller's "I'm Gonna Sit Right Down and Write Myself a Letter." Frank Sinatra's professional singing career began when he won a 6-month contract to perform on stage and radio across the U.S., first prize from the radio program *Major Bowes Amateur Hour.*

SPORTS: Baseball: The AL's Detroit Tigers defeated the NL's Chicago Cubs 4 games to 2 in the World Series. Babe Ruth hit 3 home runs on May 25 against the Pittsburgh Pirates, the final one being the last of his 714 career home runs. Ruth announced his retirement from baseball June 2. Football: The Detroit Lions beat the New York Giants 26-7 to win the NFL Championship. The Southern Methodist University Mustangs were college football national champions with a 12-1 record, scoring 288 points while only giving up 39 and shut out 8 of their 12 opponents. Jay Berwanger, halfback for the University of Chicago Maroons, won the first Heisman Trophy, presented annually to the nation's most outstanding college football player. Boxing: James J. Braddock defeated Max Baer to win the World Heavyweight championship title June 13 in Long Island City, New York.

THEATRE: George Gershwin's opera *Porgy and Bess,* running 4 hours, was first performed at Carnegie Hall in New York City.

1936

BIRTHS: Jim Brown (February 17) played running back for the National Football League's Cleveland Browns from 1957 to 1965. *Sporting News* magazine named him the greatest professional football player ever in 2002. Wally Amos (July 1) founded the 'Famous Amos' chocolate chip cookie company in 1975 and has written 9 self-help books including *The Cookie Never Crumbles.* Puppeteer Jim Henson (September 24) created The Muppets in 1954 and performed the characters of Kermit the Frog, Ernie, Rowlf, Dr. Teeth, and others. Actress Mary Tyler Moore (December 29) has won 7 Emmy Awards and has a statue in downtown Minneapolis, Minnesota where her 1970s TV sitcom *The Mary Tyler Moore Show* was set.

ART & ARCHITECTURE: Photojournalist Margaret Bourke-White's photograph of the Fort Peck Dam construction along the Missouri River in Montana appeared on the first cover of *Life* magazine, November 23. Sculptor Sylvia Shaw Judson produced the bronze statue *Bird Girl,* which is featured on the cover of the 1994 novel *Midnight in the Garden of Good and Evil.* Architect Frank Lloyd Wright designed the world corporate headquarters building of Johnson Wax in Racine, Wisconsin.

FILM: *The Great Ziegfeld* starring William Powell and Myrna Loy won the Best Picture Academy Award. Other top films were *San Francisco* starring Clark Gable and Jeanette MacDonald; *Modern Times* starring Charlie Chaplin; *Libeled Lady* starring Spencer Tracy and Jean Harlow; *The Charge of the Light Brigade* starring Errol Flynn and Olivia de Havilland; and *Camille* starring Greta Garbo. Lloyd Bridges, Anthony Quinn, and Michael Redgrave made their film debuts.

INDUSTRY: With an initial investment of $350 from the sale of a used car, businessman Bob Wian started the Big Boy family restaurant chain as a 10-stool hamburger stand in Glendale, California. He sold the chain to the Mariott Corporation in 1967 for $7 million. The Solo Cup Company was founded in Lake Forest, Illinois. The iconic red plastic cups are used in American college and university games such as 'beer pong' and 'flip cup.'

LITERATURE: *Gone with the Wind,* Margaret Mitchell's Pulitzer-Prize winning epic novel about the American Civil War and its subsequent reconstruction, was published. According to a 2008 Harris Poll, it is the second favorite book for American readers (behind the Bible).

MUSIC: Popular songs included Bing Crosby's "Pennies From Heaven;" Fred Astaire's "The Way You Look Tonight;" Billie Holiday's "Summertime;" Robert Johnson's "Cross Road Blues" and "Sweet Home Chicago;" Tommy Dorsey's "Alone;" and Benny Goodman's "Glory of Love."

SPORTS: Baseball: The AL's New York Yankees defeated the NL's New York Giants 4 games to 2 in the World Series. Ty Cobb, Babe Ruth, Honus Wagner, Christy Mathewson, and Walter Johnson were the first players elected into Major League Baseball's Hall of Fame. Football: The Green Bay Packers beat the Boston Redskins 21-6 to win the NFL Championship. The University of Minnesota Golden Gophers were college football national champions with a 7-1 record. Hockey: The Detroit Red Wings won their first Stanley Cup by beating the Toronto Maple Leafs 3 games to 1. Boxing: In one of the sport's all-time biggest upsets, Max Schmeling knocked out Joe Louis at 2:29 of round 12 at New York's Yankee Stadium.

1937

BIRTHS: Actor Jack Nicholson (April 22) has had 12 Academy Award nominations, winning Best Actor twice: for *One Flew Over the Cuckoo's Nest* in 1975 and *As Good As It Gets* in 1997; as well as Best Supporting Actor for 1983's *Terms of Endearment*. Racecar driver Richard Petty (July 2) holds many NASCAR racing records including 200 career wins (27 of which came in the 1967 season alone) and 7 Daytona 500 victories. Comedian Bill Cosby (July 12) has won 3 Emmy Awards and 9 Grammy Awards for the TV series *I Spy, Fat Albert and the Cosby Kids,* and *The Cosby Show,* as well as comedy albums. Author Hunter S. Thompson (July 18) created 'gonzo journalism,' a style of reporting that included himself in the story, in such works as the 1971 novel *Fear and Loathing in Las Vegas.*

ARCHITECTURE: When the Golden Gate Bridge opened in San Francisco, California on May 27 it was the longest suspension bridge in the world at 8,981 feet and had the world's tallest suspension towers at 692 feet above the bay. There are 80,000 miles of wire in the 2 main cables that support the roadway and 1.2 million rivets in the bridge.

FILM & RADIO: *The Life of Emile Zola* starring Paul Muni won the Best Picture Academy Award. Other top films were *Saratoga* starring Clark Gable and Jean Harlow; *Topper* starring Cary Grant and Constance Bennett; *Captains Courageous* starring Spencer Tracy; *Stella Dallas* starring Barbara Stanwyk; and Walt Disney's *Snow White and the Seven Dwarfs.* Glenn Ford, Lana Turner, and Ronald Reagan made their film debuts. Radio reporter Herbert Morrison delivered his now famous "Oh, the humanity" description of the Hindenburg disaster on May 6 in Lakehurst, New Jersey.

INDUSTRY: Vernon Rudolph started the Krispy Kreme chain of doughnut stores in Paducah, Kentucky with a secret recipe for yeast-raised doughnuts that he delivered to local grocery stores by bicycle. Ray-Ban sunglasses were originally developed for the U.S. Army Air Corps. Its famous 'Aviator' model went on sale to the public May 7. Stuckey's roadside convenience store chain was founded in Eastman, Georgia.

LITERATURE: Published works include John Steinbeck's *Of Mice and Men;* Ernest Hemingway's *To Have and Have Not;* and J.R.R. Tolkien's *The Hobbit.*

MUSIC: Popular songs included Duke Ellington's "Caravan;" Count Basie's "One O'Clock Jump;" Tommy Dorsey's "Once in a While;" Bing Crosby's "Sweet Leilani;" and Sonny Boy Williamson's "Good Morning, School Girl."

SPORTS: Baseball: The AL's New York Yankees defeated the NL's New York Giants 4 games to 1 in the World Series. Cy Young, Tris Speaker, and Nap Lajoie were added to the initial group of baseball Hall of Fame members. Football: The Washington Redskins beat the Chicago Bears 28-21 to win the NFL Championship. The University of Pittsburgh Panthers were college football national champions with a 9-0 record. Hockey: The Detroit Red Wings defeated the New York Rangers 3 games to 0 to win the Stanley Cup. Horse Racing: War Admiral won the Kentucky Derby, the Preakness Stakes, and the Belmont Stakes to claim the Triple Crown. Tennis: The U.S. beat Great Britain 5-0 to win the Davis Cup at Centre Court, Wimbledon.

THEATRE: Richard Rodgers and Lorenz Hart's musical *Babes in Arms* opened on Broadway and introduced the pop standards "Where or When," "My Funny Valentine," and "The Lady Is a Tramp."

1938

BIRTHS: Blues singer Etta James (January 25) is ranked number 22 on *Rolling Stone* magazine's list of the 100 Greatest Singers of All Time. Evel Knievel (October 17) was a motorcycle daredevil rider who holds the world record for 'most bones broken in a lifetime' with 433. Ted Turner (November 19) founded cable TV's first 24-hour news network, CNN, in 1980 and is the former owner of Major League Baseball's Atlanta Braves. He donated $1 billion to the United Nations from 1997 to 2007. Actor Jon Voight (December 29) has starred in such films as *Midnight Cowboy, Deliverance, Coming Home* (for which he won the 1978 Best Actor Academy Award), and *The Champ.* He is the father of actress Angelina Jolie.

FILM & RADIO: *You Can't Take It with You* starring James Stewart and Jean Arthur won the Best Picture Academy Award. Other top films were *The Adventures of Robin Hood* starring Errol Flynn and Olivia de Havilland; *Boys Town* starring Spencer Tracy and Mickey Rooney; *Jezebel* starring Bette Davis and Henry Fonda; and *Sweethearts* starring Jeanette MacDonald and Nelson Eddy. William Holden, Vincent Price, and John Garfield made their film debuts. Orson Welles directed and narrated the live radio drama *The War of the Worlds* October 30 on the CBS Radio network. The first two thirds of the 60-minute broadcast were presented as a series of simulated news bulletins, which suggested to many listeners that an actual alien invasion by Martians was currently in progress. Kate Smith sang "God Bless America" for the first time on her radio show November 10, the day before Armistice Day.

INDUSTRY: The Topps Company, a leading producer of collectible sports cards, was founded in Brooklyn, New York. Mac Tools professional hand tool company started in Westerville, Ohio. The Columbia Sportswear Company was founded by current chairwoman Gert Boyle's parents in Beaverton, Oregon. The company was named for the nearby Columbia River. Edelbrock, a specialty performance automotive and motorcycle aftermarket parts manufacturer, was founded in Beverly Hills, California.

MUSIC: Popular songs included Fred Astaire's "Nice Work If You Can Get It;" Bob Hope & Shirley Ross' "Thanks For the Memory;" Hoagy Carmichael's "Heart and Soul;" Ella Fitzgerald's "A-Tisket, A-Tasket;" Louis Armstrong's "Jeepers Creepers;" The Seven Dwarfs "Whistle While You Work;" and Harry Warren's "You Must Have Been a Beautiful Baby." Benny Goodman played the first jazz concert held at Carnegie Hall on January 16.

SPORTS: Baseball: The AL's New York Yankees swept the NL's Chicago Cubs 4 games to 0 in the World Series. Cincinnati Reds pitcher Johnny Vander Meer became the only player in baseball history to throw back-to-back no-hitters in consecutive starts. Pitcher Grover Cleveland Alexander was added to the inaugural class of baseball's Hall of Fame. Football: The New York Giants beat the Green Bay Packers 23-17 to win the NFL Championship. The Texas Christian University Horned Frogs were college football national champions with a 10-0 record.

THEATRE: Thornton Wilder's Pulitzer Prize winning play *Our Town* opened January 22 at the McCarter Theater in Princeton, New Jersey.

1939

BIRTHS: Francis Ford Coppola (April 7) is best known for directing the films *The Godfather* (parts I and II), and *Apocalypse Now*. He is the father of director Sofia Coppola and the uncle of actor Nicolas Cage. Comedienne Lily Tomlin (September 1) has won 2 Tony Awards for her work on Broadway, a 1972 Grammy Award for Best Comedy Album, and an Emmy Award for her work on TV. Fashion designer Ralph Lauren (October 14) founded the upscale clothing company, Polo Ralph Lauren, in 1967. Record producer Phil Spector (December 26) pioneered the girl group sound of the early 1960s and produced The Beatles' final album, *Let It Be* in 1970. In 2009 Spector began serving a life sentence for the murder of actress Lana Clarkson.

ART: Sculptor James Earle Fraser created the bronze *Equestrian Statue of Theodore Roosevelt,* which is located at the American Museum of Natural History in New York City. Originator of the mobile kinetic sculpture, Alexander Calder created his steel wire and aluminum mobile, *Lobster Trap and Fish Tail,* which hangs in New York's Museum of Modern Art. The comic book superhero Batman, created by artist Bob Kane, first appeared in *Detective Comics #27*.

FILM: Motion picture historians often rate 1939 as 'the greatest year in the history of Hollywood.' *Gone with the Wind* won 10 Academy Awards, including Best Picture, Best Director for Victor Fleming, Best Actress for Vivian Leigh, and Best Supporting Actress for Hattie McDaniel (the first African-American to win an Academy Award). Other top films were *The Wizard of Oz* starring Judy Garland; *Ninotchka* starring Greta Garbo; *Mr. Smith Goes to Washington* starring James Stewart; *Stagecoach* directed by John Ford and starring John Wayne; *Goodbye, Mr. Chips* starring Robert Donat and Greer Garson; *The Old Maid* starring Bette Davis and Miriam Hopkins; and *Jesse James* starring Henry Fonda and Tyrone Power. Maureen O'Hara and Veronica Lake made their film debuts.

INDUSTRY: Archie Comics, Atlas Comics, and Marvel Comics were all founded in 1939. The Sara Lee Corporation, maker of frozen and packaged foods, was founded in Baltimore, Maryland. Bill Hewlett and David Packard started the Hewlett-Packard Company in a one-car garage in Palo Alto, California. It is now the world's largest personal computer manufacturer.

LITERATURE: Works published include John Steinbeck's Pulitzer Prize winning novel *The Grapes of Wrath,* Ernest Hemingway's *The Snows of Kilimanjaro,* and Raymond Chandler's *The Big Sleep.*

MUSIC: Popular songs included Judy Garland's "Over the Rainbow;" Glenn Miller's "Moonlight Serenade;" Kate Smith's "God Bless America;" Billie Holiday's "Strange Fruit;" and Louis Armstrong's "When the Saints Go Marching In."

SPORTS: Baseball: The AL's New York Yankees swept the NL's Cincinnati Reds 4 games to 0 in the World Series. George Sisler, Eddie Collins, and Willie Keeler joined the inaugural class as the National Baseball Hall of Fame opened June 12 in Cooperstown, New York. Football: The Green Bay Packers beat the New York Giants 27-0 to win the NFL Championship. The Agricultural and Mechanical College of Texas (Texas A&M) Aggies were college football national champions with a 10-0 record.

1940

On April 1, the U.S. population was 132,164,569 people. The average yearly income for a U.S. worker was $1,286, equal to $20,056 today; the average house cost $7,211, equal to $112,458 today; the average car cost $850, equal to $13,256 today; a gallon of gas cost 19 cents, equal to $2.96 today; and a bicycle cost $29, equal to $452 today.

BIRTHS: Professional golfer Jack Nicklaus (January 21) holds the record for the most major golf championship wins with 18, among 115 worldwide titles. His book *Golf My Way* is the best-selling golf instructional book ever. Ricky Nelson (May 8) starred with his real life family on TV's *The Adventures of Ozzie and Harriet* from 1952 to 1966 and placed 53 songs on the billboard Hot 100 charts as a singer-songwriter. Drag racer Shirley Muldowney (June 19) was the first woman to receive a National Hot Rod Association (NHRA) license and won the Top Fuel championship title in 1977, 1980, and 1982. Artist Chuck Close (July 5) is best known for his large scale, photorealist portraits of politicians and celebrities.

ART: Grandma Moses' first solo exhibition, 'What a Farm Wife Painted,' opened in New York City. Howard Chandler Christy painted his massive 30-by-20-foot *Scene at the Signing of the Constitution of the United States*, which now hangs in the U.S. House of Representatives. Edward Hopper painted *Office at Night,* currently owned by and displayed at the Walker Art Center in Minneapolis, Minnesota.

FILM & TV: *Rebecca* won the Best Picture Academy Award. Other top films were *Pinocchio; Fantasia* (the first film to be released in stereo, featuring 'Fantasound', an early form of surround sound)*; Boom Town;* and *Strange Cargo.* Bugs Bunny made his film debut in the cartoon, *A Wild Hare.* Tom and Jerry first appeared in the cartoon *Puss Gets the Boot.* New York City's Madison Square Garden featured both the first ice hockey game to be televised in the U.S., between the New York Rangers and the Montreal Canadiens; and the first basketball game broadcast on TV, Fordham University vs. The University of Pittsburgh.

INDUSTRY: The first McDonald's restaurant opened in San Bernardino, California. Oldsmobile's Series 90 Custom Cruiser introduced the Hydra-Matic, the first fully automatic transmission available for cars in the U.S.

MUSIC: Popular songs from 1940 were Glenn Miller's "In the Mood;" Artie Shaw's "Frenesi;" Bing Crosby's "Only Forever;" Tommy Dorsey's "I'll Never Smile Again;" and Cliff Edwards' "When You Wish Upon a Star;" from the film *Pinocchio*. *Billboard Magazine* released its first music popularity chart.

SPORTS: Baseball: The NL's Cincinnati Reds defeated the AL's Detroit Tigers 4 games to 3 in the World Series. Football: The Chicago Bears won the NFL Championship game 73-0 over the Washington Redskins, the most lopsided victory in NFL history. It was also the first NFL title game to be broadcast on radio nationwide. Basketball: The Akron Firestone Non-Skids won the NBL Championship 3 games to 2 over the Oshgosh All-Stars. Hockey: The New York Rangers beat the Toronto Maple Leafs 4 games to 2 to win the NHL's Stanley Cup. Tennis: Don McNeill defeated Bobby Riggs to win the American Men's Singles Championship. Alice Marble defeated Helen Jacobs to win the American Women's Singles Championship. Auto Racing: Wilbur Shaw won the Indy 500 auto race. He served as president of the Indianapolis Motor Speedway from 1945 until his death in 1954.

1941

BIRTHS: Pete Rose (April 14) is a retired Major League Baseball player who holds the all time career records for most hits (4,256) and most games played (3,562), among others. He made 17 All-Star game appearances at an unequaled 5 different positions. Musician Bob Dylan (May 24) has received 11 Grammy Awards, 1 Academy Award, and the Presidential Medal of Freedom. Dancer Twyla Tharp (July 1) choreographed the films *Hair, Ragtime, Amadeus, White Nights,* and *I'll Do Anything.* Sculptor Dale Chihuly (September 30) founded the Pilchuck Glass School near Stanwood, Washington and established the Rhode Island School of Design's glassblowing program.

FILM & TV: *Sergeant York* won the Best Picture Academy Award. Other top films were *How Green Was My Valley; Buck Privates; Tobacco Road;* and *Citizen Kane,* ranked by many as the greatest film of all time. Charlton Heston, Ava Gardner, Bruce Lee, and Deborah Kerr made their film debuts.
Commercial television began in the U.S. on July 1 with NBC and CBS launching channels in New York City. The first TV commercial occurred before a Brooklyn Dodgers baseball game and featured a 10-second spot for Bulova watches. It showed a picture of a clock superimposed on a map of the U.S. with a voice-over saying, "America runs on Bulova time."

INDUSTRY: The Jeep brand of Sport Utility Vehicles originally supplied light 4-wheel-drive vehicles to the U.S. Army during World War II. The name Jeep comes from the phonetic pronunciation of the military designation GP, which stands for Government or General Purpose. Carls Jr., the fifth largest U.S. fast food restaurant chain by number of locations, began with $311 and one hot dog cart in Anaheim, California.

LITERATURE: The first *Curious George* children's book, written and illustrated by husband and wife H.A. and Margaret Rey, was published in New York City. F. Scott Fitzgerald's unfinished novel, *The Last Tycoon,* was edited and published by Edmund Wilson a year after Fitzgerald's death.

MUSIC: Popular songs included Glenn Miller's "Chattanooga Choo Choo;" Billie Holiday's "God Bless the Child;" Duke Ellington's "Take the 'A' Train;" The Andrew Sisters' "Boogie Woogie Bugle Boy;" Ernest Tubbs' "Walking the Floor Over You;" Fred Astaire's "So Near and Yet So Far;" and Jimmy Dorsey's "Green Eyes." Les Paul designed and built the first electric guitar.

SPORTS: Baseball: The AL's New York Yankees defeated the NL's Brooklyn Dodgers 4 games to 1 in the World Series. The Yankees Joe DiMaggio had a Major League Baseball record 56-game hitting streak from May 15 to July 16. Boston Red Sox left fielder Ted Williams recorded a season batting average of .406, the last time anyone has hit over .400 for a season. Football: The Chicago Bears beat the New York Giants 37-9 to win the NFL Championship. The University of Minnesota Golden Gophers were college football national champions with a record of 8-0. Minnesota halfback Bruce Smith won the Heisman Trophy. Golf: Craig Wood won the Masters Tournament in Augusta, Georgia as its first wire-to-wire champion, and the U.S. Open at Colonial Country Club in Fort Worth, Texas. Horse Racing: Whirlaway won the Kentucky Derby, the Preakness Stakes, and the Belmont Stakes to capture the Triple Crown.

1942

BIRTHS: Muhammad Ali (January 17) won boxing's 1960 Olympic gold medal and rose to cultural icon status as World Heavyweight Champion during the 1970s. He was named 'Sportsman of the Century' by *Sports Illustrated* magazine in 1999. Author Michael Crichton (October 23) became the only creative artist ever to chart works at number one simultaneously in TV with *ER*, film with *Jurassic Park*, and book sales with *Disclosure,* in 1994. Fashion designer Calvin Klein (November 19) founded his own fashion house in 1968 in New York City. Musician Jimi Hendrix (November 27) is a member of the rock and roll hall of fame and is widely considered to be the greatest electric guitarist in music history.

ART & PHOTOGRAPHY: Edward Hopper produced his most famous work, *Nighthawks,* a realist painting that portrays people sitting in a downtown diner late at night. Within months of its completion, it was sold to the Art Institute of Chicago for $3,000, and has remained there ever since. *The Detroit News* reporter Milton Brooks' photograph titled *Ford Strikes Riot* won the first Pulitzer Prize in Photography.

FILM & TV: *Mrs. Miniver* won the Best Picture Academy Award. Other top films were *Bambi; For Me and My Gal; Cat People;* and *To the Shores of Tripoli.* Elizabeth Taylor, Gene Kelly, Harry Morgan, and the cartoon characters Mighty Mouse and Tweety Bird made their debuts. The U.S. War Production Board halted the manufacture of television and radio equipment for consumer use on April 1; the ban was lifted October 1, 1945. The FCC minimum programming time required of U.S. TV stations was cut from 15 hours to 4 hours a week during World War II.

INDUSTRY: Freightliner Trucks, an American manufacturer of semi-trailer trucks, was founded in Portland, Oregon. All Chrysler, Ford, and General Motors automotive plants were converted to military production.

LITERATURE: Works published include Raymond Chandler's *The High Window;* Robert Heinlein's *Beyond This Horizon;* John Steinbeck's *The Moon is Down;* and Evelyn Waugh's *Put Out More Flags. The New York Times* newspaper launched its influential New York Times Best Seller List.

MUSIC: Popular songs were Bing Crosby's "White Christmas," which has become the best selling single of all time with sales of over 50 million copies worldwide; Glenn Miller's "Moonlight Cocktail;" Frank Sinatra's "Night and Day;" The Andrew Sisters' "Don't Sit Under The Apple Tree;" and Jimmy Dorsey's "Tangerine." Johnny Mercer founded Capitol Records in Los Angeles, California.

SPORTS: Baseball: The NL's St. Louis Cardinals defeated the AL's New York Yankees 4 games to 1 in the World Series. The Kansas City Monarchs swept the Homestead Grays 4 games to 0 in the Negro League World Series. Rogers Hornsby was elected to the Baseball Hall of Fame, receiving 78% of the vote. Football: The Washington Redskins won the NFL championship game 14-6 over the Chicago Bears. The Ohio State University Buckeyes were college football national champions with a 9-1 record. Basketball: The Oshkosh All-Stars beat the Fort Wayne Zollner Pistons 2 games to 1 to win the NBL Championship. The Stanford University Indians defeated the Dartmouth Big Green 53-38 to become college basketball champions.

1943

BIRTHS: Rock and Roll Hall of Fame member Janis Joplin (January 19) was ranked #28 on *Rolling Stone* magazine's list of the 100 Greatest Singers of All Time. Quarterback Joe Namath (May 31) was the MVP of Super Bowl III when his New York Jets defeated the heavily favored Baltimore Colts 16-7 in Miami, Florida. He was elected to the NFL's Pro Football Hall of Fame in 1985. Playwright, actor, and director Sam Shepard (November 5) won the 1979 Pulitzer Prize for Drama for his play *Buried Child.* Billie Jean King (November 22) is an International Tennis Hall of Fame Member who won 12 Grand Slam tennis titles among her 129 career tournament wins.

ART & ARCHITECTURE: Edward Hopper created his oil on canvas realist painting *Hotel Lobby,* which is displayed by the Indianapolis Museum of Art in Indiana. *Four Freedoms* is a series of oil paintings produced by Norman Rockwell that were printed in *The Saturday Evening Post* magazine. The Jefferson Memorial, honoring the 3rd U.S. President Thomas Jefferson, opened in Washington, D.C. The headquarters of the U.S. Department of Defense and the world's largest office building by floor area, The Pentagon, opened in Arlington County, Virginia.

FILM & RADIO: *Casablanca* won the Best Picture Academy Award. Other top films were *For Whom the Bell Tolls; A Guy Named Joe; Girl Crazy;* and *The Song of Bernadette,* which won the first Golden Globe Award for Best Picture. Robert Mitchum, Frank Sinatra, and Shelley Winters made their film debuts. Edward R. Murrow delivered his famous 'Orchestrated Hell' broadcast on CBS radio December 3, describing his firsthand experience with a Royal Air Force nighttime bombing raid on Berlin, Germany during World War II.

INDUSTRY: The American Broadcasting Company (ABC) was created in New York City. Pizzeria restaurant chain Uno Chicago Grill is where the Chicago style, deep-dish pizza originated. Jo-Ann Stores, a retail craft and fabric supply store chain, was founded in Cleveland, Ohio.

LITERATURE: Works published include Betty Smith's first novel, *A Tree Grows in Brooklyn;* Esther Forbes' Newbery Medal winning children's novel, *Johnny Tremain;* Ayn Rand's *The Fountainhead,* which has sold over 6.5 million copies worldwide; and H. P. Lovecraft's science fiction, fantasy, and horror collection *Beyond the Wall of Sleep.*

MUSIC: Popular songs were The Mills Brothers' "Paper Doll;" Glenn Miller's "That Old Black Magic;" The Ink Spots' "Don't Get Around Much Anymore;" Lena Horne's "Stormy Weather;" and Dick Haymes' " You'll Never Know." Duke Ellington performed at New York City's Carnegie Hall for the first time, premiering his most famous jazz symphony, *Black, Brown, and Beige.*

SPORTS: Baseball: The AL's New York Yankees defeated the NL's St. Louis Cardinals 4 games to 1 in the World Series. Football: The Chicago Bears beat the Washington Redskins 41-26 to win the NFL Championship. The University of Notre Dame Fighting Irish were college football's national champions with a 9-1 record and its quarterback Angelo Bertelli won the Heisman Trophy. Basketball: The Sheboygan Redskins defeated the Fort Wayne Zollner Pistons 2 games to 1 to win the NBL Championship.

THEATRE: Richard Rodgers and Oscar Hammerstein II's Broadway musical *Oklahoma!* ran for an unprecedented 2,243 performances at the the St. James Theatre from March 31, 1943 until May 29, 1948, grossing $7 million.

1944

BIRTHS: Author Alice Walker (February 9) is best known for her novel *The Color Purple,* for which she won the Pulitzer Prize for Fiction and the National Book Award in 1983. Singer Diana Ross (March 26) was the lead singer for the Motown group The Supremes and was named 'Female Entertainer of the Century' by *Billboard* magazine in 1976 for her 18 #1 U.S. hit singles. Steve Fossett (April 22) was a businessman and adventurer who became the first person to fly solo nonstop around the world in a balloon in 2002. Frank Oz (May 25) is known for creating and performing the characters Miss Piggy and Fozzie Bear on TV's *The Muppet Show* as well as Cookie Monster, Bert, and Grover on *Sesame Street*.

FILM & RADIO: *Going My Way* won 7 Academy Awards, including Best Picture and the Best Actor Oscar for Bing Crosby. Other top films were *Meet Me in St. Louis* starring Judy Garland; *Since You Went Away* starring Claudette Colbert and Shirley Temple; *Double Indemnity* starring Fred MacMurray and Barbara Stanwyck; *Pin Up Girl* starring Betty Grable; and *Hollywood Canteen* starring Bette Davis and Joan Crawford. Lauren Bacall, Gregory Peck, Jean Simmons, and Angela Lansbury made their film debuts. The radio program *The Adventures of Ozzie and Harriet* starring the real life Nelson family premiered on October 8.

INDUSTRY: The original Chiquita Banana animated mascot was created by cartoonist Dik Browne, best known for writing and drawing the *Hagar the Horrible* comic strip.

MUSIC: Popular songs included Bing Crosby's "Swinging on a Star" and "I'll Be Seeing You;" Leadbelly's "Goodnight Irene;" Jo Stafford's "It Could Happen To You;" The Mills Brothers' "You Always Hurt the One You Love;" Cole Porter's "Don't Fence Me In;" Jimmy Dorsey's "Besame Mucho;" and Buck Ram's "Twilight Time."

SPORTS: Baseball: The NL's St. Louis Cardinals defeated the AL's St. Louis Browns 4 games to 2 in the World Series. On June 10, 15-year old Joe Nuxhall, a pitcher for the Cincinnati Reds, became the youngest player in Major League Baseball history to appear in a game. Football: The Green Bay Packers beat the New York Giants 14-7 at the Polo Grounds in New York City to win the NFL Championship. The Army Black Knights, representing the U.S. Military Academy, were college football national champions with a 9-0 record. Ohio State University Quarterback Les Horvath won the Heisman Trophy. Basketball: The Fort Wayne Zollner Pistons swept the Sheboygan Redskins 3 games to 0 to win the NBL Championship. The University of Utah Utes won their first college basketball national championship by beating the Dartmouth College Big Green 42-40 in the title game at New York City's Madison Square Garden.

THEATRE: Mary Chase's Pulitzer Prize winning play *Harvey* ran on Broadway for 1,775 performances over nearly 5 years. Tennessee Williams' play *The Glass Managerie* premiered in Chicago. The musical *On the Town* introduced the song "New York, New York," written by Leonard Bernstein.

1945

BIRTHS: Debbie Harry (July 1) was the lead singer for the pioneering punk and new wave rock band Blondie and has acted in more than 30 films. Jerry Bruckheimer (September 21) has produced such hit films as *Beverly Hills Cop, Top Gun,* and *Pearl Harbor,* as well as the hit TV shows *CSI: Crime Scene Investigation* and *The Amazing Race.* Henry Winkler (October 30) was ranked #4 on *TV Guide's* 1999 list of the '50 Greatest TV Characters of All Time' for his portrayal of Arthur 'Fonzie' Fonzarelli on the 1970s TV sitcom *Happy Days.* Actress Goldie Hawn (November 21) won the 1969 Best Supporting Actress Academy Award for the film *Cactus Flower.* She is the mother of actress Kate Hudson and has been in a relationship with actor Kurt Russell since 1983.

ART: Associated Press photographer Joe Rosenthal took the Pulitzer Prize winning photograph *Raising the Flag on Iwo Jima* during World War II's Battle of Iwo Jima on February 23. Artist Elizabeth Shoumatoff was in the process of painting President Franklin D. Roosevelt's portrait at his personal retreat in Warm Springs, Georgia on April 12 when the President collapsed, lost consciousness, and died 3 hours later from a massive cerebral hemorrhage. *The Unfinished Portrait of Franklin D. Roosevelt* hangs at the retreat known as the Little White House.

FILM: *The Lost Weekend* won the Best Picture Academy Award as well as the Best Director Oscar and the Best Screenplay for Billy Wilder, and the Best Actor Oscar for Ray Milland. Other top films were *The Bells of St. Mary's* starring Bing Crosby and Ingrid Bergman; *Anchors Aweigh* starring Gene Kelly and Frank Sinatra; *Spellbound* starring Gregory Peck and Ingrid Bergman; *Leave Her to Heaven* starring Gene Tierney and Cornel Wilde; *The Dolly Sisters* starring Betty Grable and June Haver; and *Mildred Pierce* starring Joan Crawford, for which she won the Best Actress Academy Award.

INDUSTRY: Mattel, the world's largest toy company based on revenue, gets its name from the 2 founders: Harold '**Matt**' Matson and **El**liot Handler. Its products include the Barbie Doll (invented by Ruth Handler, Elliot's wife, and named for their daughter Barbara), Fisher Price, Hot Wheels, and Matchbox toys. The largest sausage company in the U.S., Johnsonville Foods, was founded in Johnsonville, Wisconsin. Minute Maid was the first company to produce orange juice concentrate, allowing it to be distributed throughout the U.S. and served year-round.

MUSIC: Popular songs included Doris Day's "Sentimental Journey;" The Andrew Sisters' "Rum and Coca-Cola;" Perry Como's "Till the End of Time;" Johnny Mercer and Jo Stafford's "Candy;" and Harry James' "If I Loved You."

SPORTS: Baseball: The AL's Detroit Tigers defeated the NL's Chicago Cubs 4 games to 3 in the World Series. Football: The Cleveland Rams beat the Washington Redskins 15-14 to win the NFL Championship. The Army Cadets won their second consecutive college football national championship with a 9-0 record. Golfer Byron Nelson won 11 consecutive tournaments and 18 total tournaments in 1945.

THEATRE: The Broadway musical *Carousel,* written by Richard Rogers and Oscar Hammerstein II, opened April 19 and ran for 890 performances. In 1999, *Time* magazine named it the best musical of the 20th century.

1946

BIRTHS: Dolly Parton (January 19) is a country music star who has written over 3,000 songs including "I Will Always Love You," "Jolene," and "9 to 5." She has sold an estimated 100 million albums worldwide. Robert Mapplethorpe (November 4) was a photographer known for his large-scale, highly stylized black and white portraits. Actress Sally Field (November 6) started her career in the TV series *Gidget* and *The Flying Nun* before winning 2 Best Actress Academy Awards for her performances in 1979's *Norma Rae* and 1984's *Places in the Heart*. Steven Spielberg (December 18) has directed such films as *Jaws, Saving Private Ryan, E.T. the Extra Terrestrial, Schindler's List,* and *Jurassic Park*. His movies have made more than $8.5 billion worldwide and he has a personal wealth of $3 billion.

FILM: *The Best Years of Our Lives* won the Best Picture Academy Award as well as the Best Director Oscar for William Wyler, the Best Actor Oscar for Fredric March, and the Best Supporting Actor Oscar for Harold Russell. Other top films were *Duel in the Sun* starring Gregory Peck and Jennifer Jones; *The Postman Always Rings Twice* starring Lana Turner and John Garfield; *Blue Skies* starring Bing Crosby and Fred Astaire; *Gilda* starring Rita Hayworth and Glenn Ford; *The Yearling* starring Gregory Peck and Jane Wyman; *Notorious* starring Cary Grant and Ingrid Bergman; and *The Razor's Edge* starring Tyrone Power and Gene Tierney. Kirk Douglas, Burt Lancaster, Natalie Wood, and Dean Martin made their film debuts.

INDUSTRY: Clarence Leonidas 'Leo' Fender founded the Fender Electric Instrument Company in Fullerton, California. Its famous products include the Telecaster and Stratocaster electric guitars and the Precision and Jazz bass guitars. Animal nutritionist Paul Iams founded the Iams Pet Food Company in Dayton, Ohio. He created the world's first dry dog food and called it Iams 999. James Bullough Lansing founded the JBL audio electronics company, whose primary products are loudspeakers. Aloha Airlines began service on July 26 with a single Douglas C-47 (DC-3) airplane on a flight from Honolulu, Hawaii to Maui and Hilo, Hawaii. The chicken sandwich fast food restaurant chain, Chick-fil-A, was founded in Atlanta, Georgia. Unlike most fast food chains, Chick-fil-A is closed on Sundays due to its founder's strong Christian beliefs. The Avis Rent a Car Company started with 3 cars at Willow Run Airport in Ypsilanti, Michigan.

MUSIC: Popular songs included Perry Como's "Prisoner of Love;" Frank Sinatra's "Five Minutes More;" The Ink Spots' "To Each His Own;" Nat King Cole's "(I Love You) For Sentimental Reasons;" Dinah Shore's "Laughing On The Outside;" and Vaughn Monroe's "Let it Snow! Let it Snow! Let it Snow!"

SPORTS: Baseball: The NL's St. Louis Cardinals defeated the AL's Boston Red Sox 4 games to 3 in the World Series. Football: The Chicago Bears beat the New York Giants 24-14 to win the NFL Championship. The University of Notre Dame Fighting Irish were college football national champions with a 9-0-1 record. Army halfback Glenn Davis won the Heisman Trophy.

THEATRE: Irving Berlin's musical *Annie Get Your Gun* opened on Broadway May 16 at the Imperial Theater and ran for 1,147 performances. It starred Ethel Merman as Annie and introduced the hit songs "There's No Business Like Show Business," "Anything You Can Do," and "They Say It's Wonderful."

1947

BIRTHS: Nolan Ryan (January 31) is a former Major League Baseball pitcher who holds several career records including most seasons played (27), most strikeouts (5,714), and most no-hitters (7). Actress Farrah Fawcett (February 2) starred in the 1970s TV series *Charlie's Angels.* Her 1976 poster has sold over 12 million copies and helped inspire a popular hairstyle known as 'The Farrah.' Kareem Abdul-Jabbar (April 16) is the National Basketball Association's all-time leading scorer, with 38,387 points. During his 20-year playing career, he won 6 NBA Championship titles and a record 6 regular season Most Valuable Player awards. Author Stephen King (September 21) writes horror, suspense, science fiction, and fantasy books that have sold over 350 million copies.

FILM & TV: *Gentleman's Agreement* won the Best Picture Academy Award. Other top films were *Unconquered* starring Gary Cooper; *Mother Wore Tights* starring Betty Grable; *Life With Father* starring William Powell and Elizabeth Taylor; and *Road to Rio* starring Bing Crosby and Bob Hope. Marilyn Monroe, Janet Leigh, and Richard Widmark made their film debuts. The TV news program *Meet the Press* premiered November 6 on NBC and has become the longest-running TV series in American broadcast history with over 5,000 episodes, as of March 28, 2012.

INDUSTRY: Nathan Daniel founded the musical instrument manufacturer Danelectro in Red Bank, New Jersey. The company's guitars, basses, and amplifiers were sold in Sears and Montgomery Ward department stores. Famous musicians who play Daneletro products include Jimmy Page, Eric Clapton, Jack Bruce, and Mark Knopfler. The Kenner toy company was founded in Cincinnati, Ohio and was named after the street where the original corporate offices were located.

MUSIC: Popular songs included Francis Craig's "Near You;" James Baskett's "Zip-a-Dee-Doo-Dah;" Gene Autry's "Here Comes Santa Claus;" Roy Brown's "Good Rockin' Tonight;" and Merle Travis' "Sixteen Tons." Ahmet Ertegun founded Atlantic Records, which specialized in Jazz, Rhythm and Blues, Soul, and Rock and Roll recording artists including Ray Charles, Aretha Franklin, Otis Redding, Cream, Led Zeppelin, and The Rolling Stones.

SPORTS: Baseball: The AL's New York Yankees defeated the NL's Brooklyn Dodgers 4 games to 3 in the World Series. Jackie Robinson became the first African-American player in Major League Baseball when he debuted for the Brooklyn Dodgers April 15 at Ebbets Field. The first College Baseball World Series featured the University of California Golden Bears beating the Yale University Bulldogs 2 games to 0 in the best of 3 series. Future U.S. President George Bush was captain and played first base for Yale. Football: The Chicago Cardinals defeated the Philadelphia Eagles 28-21 to win the NFL Championship. Basketball: The Philadelphia Warriors won the first NBA Championship 4 games to 1 over the Chicago Stags.

THEATRE: Tennessee Williams' Pulitzer Prize winning play *A Streetcar Named Desire* opened on Broadway starring Marlon Brando, Jessica Tandy, Kim Hunter, and Karl Malden. The first Tony Awards were held in New York City with Jose Ferrer winning best Actor-Play in *Cyrano de Bergerac* and both Ingrid Bergman in *Joan of Lorraine* and Helen Hayes in *Happy Birthday* winning Best Actress-Play.

1948

BIRTHS: Musician James Taylor (March 12) has sold 12 million U.S. copies of his 1976 *Greatest Hits* album and was inducted into the Rock and Roll Hall of Fame in 2000. Figure skater Peggy Fleming (July 27) is a 3-time World Champion and won the ladies' singles Olympic gold medal in 1968. Terry Bradshaw (September 2) won 4 Super Bowl titles as quarterback for the Pittsburgh Steelers in the 1970s and was inducted into the Pro Football Hall of Fame in 1989. Fashion designer Donna Karan (October 2) was head designer for the Anne Klein fashion house for 10 years beginning in 1974 and created the DKNY (Donna Karan New York) clothing label in 1989.

ART: Jackson Pollock produced his famous abstract expressionism oil on fiberboard painting *No. 5, 1948.* It was reportedly sold to businessman David Martinez for $140 million in 2006. This would make it the second most expensive painting ever sold, behind Paul Cezanne's *The Card Players,* sold in 2011 to the Royal Family of Qatar for $250 million.

FILM & TV: *Hamlet* became the first British film to win the Best Picture Academy Award and Laurence Olivier won the Best Actor Oscar in the title role. Other top films were *Easter Parade* starring Judy Garland and Fred Astaire; *The Treasure of the Sierra Madre* starring Humphrey Bogart; *Red River* starring John Wayne and Montgomery Clift; *The Three Musketeers* starring Gene Kelly and Lana Turner; and *Joan of Arc* starring Ingrid Bergman. Rock Hudson and Doris Day made their film debuts. Milton Berle became the first U.S. TV star with the debut of *Texaco Star Theater. The Ed Sullivan Show* premiered on CBS TV with his first guests Dean Martin and Jerry Lewis. Other TV show premieres included the first Mark Goodson-Bill Todman produced game show, *Winner Take All;* and *Candid Camera,* which was created, produced, and hosted by Allen Funt.

INDUSTRY: Makers of the Hula Hoop, Frisbee, Slip 'n Slide, Super Ball, Silly String, Hacky Sack, and Boogie Board, the Wham-O toy company was started by Richard Knerr and Arthur 'Spud' Melin in the Knerr family garage in Pasadena, California. Harry and Esther Snyder founded the In-N-Out Burger restaurant chain in Baldwin Park, California. Richard 'Dick' Stack founded Dick's Sporting Goods in Binghamton, New York at the age of 18.

MUSIC: Popular songs included Nat King Cole's "Nature Boy;" Dinah Shore's "Buttons & Bows;" Art Mooney's "I'm Looking Over a Four Leaf Clover;" Vaughn Monroe's "Cool Water;" Kay Kyser's "The Woody Woodpecker Song;" Pee Wee Hunt's "Twelfth Street Rag;" and Jo Stafford's "Red River Valley."

SPORTS: Baseball: The AL's Cleveland Indians defeated the NL's Boston Braves 4 games to 2 in the World Series. Legendary New York Yankee Babe Ruth died August 16 at the age of 53 from throat cancer. Football: The Philadelphia Eagles beat the Chicago Cardinals 7-0 in a blizzard to win the NFL Championship at Philadelphia's Shibe Park. The University of Michigan Wolverines were college football national champions with a 9-0 record. Southern Methodist University halfback Doak Walker won the Heisman Trophy. Boxing: Joe Louis knocked out Jersey Joe Walcott in the 11th round at New York's Yankee Stadium to retain his heavyweight title for an unprecedented 25th time. Shortly after the bout, Louis retired from boxing.

THEATRE: Cole Porter's Tony Award-winning musical *Kiss Me, Kate* opened at Broadway's New Century Theatre and ran for 1,077 performances.

1949

BIRTHS: Actress Meryl Streep (June 22) has received 17 Academy Award nominations, winning 3, and 26 Golden Globe nominations, winning 8, giving her the most nominations of any actor in the history of both awards. Fashion designer Vera Wang (June 27) was senior fashion editor at *Vogue* magazine for 15 years, beginning in 1972 at age 23. She is now the most prominent designer of bridal wear in the U.S. Photographer Annie Leibovitz (October 2) took the January 22, 1981 *Rolling Stone* magazine cover photo of John Lennon and Yoko Ono on the day he was murdered. Musician Tom Waits (December 7) has released 16 studio albums and composes musical scores for films. He was inducted into the Rock and Roll Hall of Fame in 2011.

ARCHITECTURE: The Glass House in New Canaan, Connecticut was designed and built by architect Philip Johnson as his own residence. The modern architectural styled project showcases minimal structure, geometry, proportion, and the effects of transparency and reflection. The modern architectural styled Eames House in the Pacific Palisades section of Los Angeles, California was designed and built by the husband and wife design pioneers Charles and Ray Eames as their home and studio.

FILM & TV: *All the King's Men* won the Best Picture Academy Award as well as the Best Actor Oscar for Broderick Crawford and the Best Supporting Actress Oscar for Mercedes McCambridge. Other top films were *Samson and Delilah* starring Victor Mature and Hedy Lamarr; *Battleground* starring Van Johnson; *Sands of Iwo Jima* starring John Wayne; *The Heiress* starring Olivia de Havilland and Montgomery Clift; *I Was a Male War Bride* starring Cary Grant and Ann Sheridan; and *Twelve O'Clock High* starring Gregory Peck. Dean Martin, Jerry Lewis, Yul Brynner, Tony Curtis, Richard Burton, and Max von Sydow made their film debuts. TV show premieres included *The Lone Ranger, Colgate Theatre,* and *Bozo the Clown.* Ventriloquist Shirley Dinsdale won the first ever Emmy Award, for 'Outstanding Television Personality.'

LITERATURE: Published works include Nelson Algren's National Book Award winning novel, *The Man with the Golden Arm,* and Shirley Jackson's *The Lottery and Other Stories,* her only collection of short stories published during her lifetime.

MUSIC: Popular songs included Vaughn Monroe's "Ghost Riders in The Sky;" Frankie Laine's "That Lucky Old Sun" and "Mule Train;" The Andrew Sisters' "I Can Dream, Can't I?;" Dinah Shore & Buddy Clark's "Baby, It's Cold Outside;" and Perry Como's "Some Enchanted Evening."

SPORTS: Baseball: The AL's New York Yankees defeated the NL's Brooklyn Dodgers 4 games to 1 in the World Series. Football: The Philadelphia Eagles beat the Los Angeles Rams 14-0 to win the NFL Championship. The University of Notre Dame Fighting Irish were college football national champions with a 9-0 record. Motor Racing: Robert 'Red' Byron, driving an Oldsmobile, was the series champion in NASCAR's first Strictly Stock season.

THEATRE: Arthur Miller's play *Death of a Salesman* won the Pulitzer Prize for Drama and the Tony Award for Best Play. Starring Lee J. Cobb as Willy Loman, the play opened at Broadway's Morosco Theatre on February 10 and ran for 742 performances.

1950

On April 1, the U.S. population was 150,697,361 people. The average yearly income for a U.S. worker was $2,686, equal to $24,406 today; the average house cost $15,796, equal to $143,530 today; the average car cost $1,480, equal to $13,448 today; a gallon of gas cost 20 cents, equal to $1.81 today; and a TV cost $199, equal to $1,809 today.

BIRTHS: Swimmer Mark Spitz (February 10) won 7 gold medals at the 1972 Olympics, setting new world records in all 7 events in which he competed. Musician Stevie Wonder (May 13) has won 22 Grammy Awards in a career that started when he signed with Motown Records at the age of 11. He continues to record for Motown today. John Landis (August 3) has directed such films as *Animal House, The Blues Brothers,* and *Coming to America,* as well as the Michael Jackson music videos *Thriller* and *Black and White.* Actress Julie Kavner (September 7) is best known for her role as Marge Simpson on the animated TV series *The Simpsons.*

FILM & TV: *All About Eve* won the Best Picture Academy Award, among a record 14 award nominations. Other top films were *Born Yesterday; Annie Get Your Gun; Destination Moon;* and *Sunset Boulevard.* James Stewart became the first Hollywood actor to receive a percentage of a film's profits along with a salary, for the film *Winchester '73.* He earned 50% of the film's profits, amounting to $600,000. Marlon Brando, James Dean, Charlton Heston, Sidney Poitier, and Debbie Reynolds made their film debuts in 1950. The Nielsen Ratings began ranking TV shows with the top shows being: 1.*Texaco Star Theater,* 2. *Fireside Theater,* 3. *Philco Television Playhouse,* and 4. *Your Show of Shows.*

INDUSTRY: The daily comic strip *Peanuts* by cartoonist Charles M. Schultz premiered in 9 U.S. newspapers on October 2. At its peak, *Peanuts* ran in over 2,600 newspapers with 355 million readers in 75 countries and a total of 17,897 strips published. Merchandise from Charlie Brown, Snoopy, and the rest of the *Peanuts* gang earned Schultz more than $1 billion. Cartoonist Mort Walker began his comic strip *Beetle Bailey* in 1950. It is considered the oldest comic strip still being produced by the original artist. Doughnut and coffee retailer Dunkin' Donuts was founded in Quincy, Massachusetts. Silly Putty began being sold in small plastic eggs. Today 20,000 eggs are sold daily worldwide and more than 300 million eggs have been sold since 1950.

LITERATURE: Author Jack Kerouac had his first novel published, *The Town and the City. The Martian Chronicles* by Ray Bradbury and *I, Robot* by Isaac Asimov are science fiction short story collections.

MUSIC: Popular songs included Nat King Cole's "Mona Lisa;" Patti Page's "Tennessee Waltz;" Phil Harris' "The Thing;" and Red Foley's "Chattanoogie Shoe Shine Boy." Record Producer Sam Phillips founded Sun Studios in Memphis, Tennessee. The first mass-produced solid body electric guitar, the *Esquire,* was introduced by the Leo Fender guitar company.

SPORTS: Baseball: The AL's New York Yankees swept the World Series 4 games to 0 over the NL's Philadelphia Phillies. Football: The Cleveland Browns beat the Los Angeles Rams 30-28 in the NFL Championship Game. Basketball: The NBA championship was won by the Minneapolis Lakers 4 games to 2 over the Syracuse Nationals. Hockey: The Detroit Red Wings won the Stanley Cup over the New York Rangers 4 games to 3. Soccer: The U.S. defeated England 1-0 in the FIFA World Cup.

1951

BIRTHS: Fashion designer Tommy Hilfiger (March 24) founded his own clothing brand company in 1984, which 20 years later had revenues of $1.8 billion and 5,400 employees. Dale Earnhardt (April 29) was a racecar driver who won 76 NASCAR races during his career. He also won 7 Winston Cup Championship Titles, which is tied with Richard Petty for the most all time. Musician Chrissie Hynde (September 7) is the lead singer-songwriter for the rock band Pretenders, who were inducted into the Rock and Roll Hall of Fame in 2005. Actor Mark Hamill (September 25) is best known for playing the film character Luke Skywalker in the original *Star Wars* trilogy.

ART & ARCHITECTURE: The 9th Street Art Exhibition in New York City helped propel avant-garde expressionism into mainstream American art, featuring the work of such artists as Willem de Kooning, Jackson Pollack, Perle Fine, and Hans Hoffmann. The Farnsworth House, designed and built by Ludwig Mies van der Rohe near Plano, Illinois, is one of the best examples of American modern architecture in the International style.

FILM, RADIO, AND TV: *An American in Paris* starring Gene Kelly and Leslie Caron won the Best Picture Academy Award. Other top films were *Quo Vadis* starring Robert Taylor and Deborah Kerr; *Show Boat* starring Ava Gardner and Howard Keel; *A Place in the Sun* starring Montgomery Clift and Elizabeth Taylor; and *A Streetcar Names Desire* starring Vivian Leigh and Marlon Brando. Audrey Hepburn, Grace Kelly, Charles Bronson, and Rod Steiger made their film debuts. *Paul Harvey News and Comment* began April 1 on the ABC Radio Network and continued for 59 years. DJ Alan Freed coined the term 'Rock 'N' Roll' on July 11, in reference to the rhythm and blues music played on his nighttime radio program on Cleveland, Ohio's WJW. *I Love Lucy* debuted on CBS Television October 15 as the first TV show to be produced on film instead of being broadcast live and made Lucille Ball the world's first female television star.

INDUSTRY: The Jack in the Box fast food restaurant chain was founded in San Diego, California. Oleg Cassini founded his own fashion brand that became famous for designing clothing for Jacqueline Kennedy, known as 'The Jackie Look.'

LITERATURE: Works published include J. D. Salinger's *The Catcher in the Rye;* James Jones' *From Here to Eternity;* Herman Wouk's *The Caine Mutiny;* and Isaac Asimov's *Foundation.* Conrad Richter's novel *The Town* won the Pulitzer Prize for Fiction.

MUSIC: Popular songs included Johnnie Ray's "Cry;" Rosemary Clooney's "Come On-a My House;" Les Paul and Mary Ford's "How High the Moon;" Perry Como's "If;" and Tony Bennett's "Because of You."

SPORTS: Baseball: Bobby Thomson of the New York Giants hit a 3-run walk-off home run, known as 'the shot heard round the world,' to beat the Brooklyn Dodgers 5-4 for the National League Title. The AL's New York Yankees defeated the NL's New York Giants 4 games to 2 in the World Series. Football: The Los Angeles Rams defeated the Cleveland Browns 24-17 to win the NFL Championship. The University of Tennessee Volunteers were college football national champions with a 10-1 record.

THEATRE: *Guys and Dolls* won the Pulitzer Prize for Drama and 5 Tony Awards, including Best Musical.

1952

BIRTHS: Author Amy Tan (February 19) is best known for her novel *The Joy Luck Club,* which has been translated into 35 languages. Country music singer George Strait (May 18) holds the world record for the most number one hit singles with 59 and is the only artist to score a top 10 single for 30 consecutive years. David Fincher (August 28) has directed such Hollywood films as *Alien 3, Seven, Fight Club, The Social Network,* and *The Girl with the Dragon Tattoo.* Jimmy Connors (September 2) won 148 professional men's tennis titles including 8 Grand Slam singles titles and 2 Grand Slam doubles titles (with Ilie Nastase).

ART & ARCHITECTURE: Jackson Pollack created his abstract painting, *Blue Poles,* considered his most famous work, which is now owned by the National Gallery of Australia in Canberra. *On the Contrary* is a surrealist painting by Kay Sage, which hangs in the Walker Art Center in Minneapolis, Minnesota. The 39-story, 505-foot tall United Nations Secretariat Building was completed in New York City. The Sands Hotel, designed by architect Wayne McAllister, was the 7th resort to open on the Las Vegas Strip.

FILM & TV: Cecil B. DeMille's *The Greatest Show on Earth* won the Best Picture Academy Award. Other top films were *High Noon* starring Gary Cooper and Grace Kelly; *Singin' in the Rain* starring Gene Kelly, Debbie Reynolds, and Donald O'Connor; *Ivanhoe* starring Robert Taylor and Joan Fontaine; and *The Quiet Man* starring John Wayne and Maureen O'Hara. Brigitte Bardot, Anne Bancroft, and Julie Harris made their film debuts. The popular TV dance and music program *American Bandstand* premiered October 7 on WFIL-TV in Philadelphia, Pennsylvania and ran until 1989.

INDUSTRY: The Holiday Inn chain of hotels was founded in Memphis, Tennessee. Ore-Ida frozen foods got its name from the first 3 letters of Oregon and Idaho, where the company grows its famous potatoes. Hasbro introduced the toy Mr. Potato Head as a collection of body parts that would pin into real potatoes. Edward Haas patented his PEZ candy dispenser modeled after a cigarette lighter.

LITERATURE: Works published include Ernest Hemingway's last major novel, *The Old Man and the Sea;* John Steinbeck's *East of Eden;* Ralph Ellison's *Invisible Man;* and the best selling children's book of all time, *Charlotte's Web,* by E.B. White.

MUSIC: Popular songs included Kay Starr's "Wheel of Fortune;" Jo Stafford's "You Belong to Me;" Frankie Laine's "High Noon (Do Not Forsake Me);" Al Martino's "Here in My Heart;" and Patti Page's "I Went To Your Wedding." The Palomino Club opened in North Hollywood, California as country music's best west coast venue with performers such as Johnny Cash and Patsy Cline.

SPORTS: The AL's New York Yankees defeated the NL's Brooklyn Dodgers 4 games to 3 in the World Series. Football: The Detroit Lions defeated the Cleveland Browns 17-7 to win the NFL Championship. The Georgia Institute of Technology Yellow Jackets were college football national champions with a 12-0 record. Basketball: The Minneapolis Lakers defeated the Syracuse Nationals 4 games to 3 to win the NBA Championship. Hockey: The Detroit Red Wings swept the Montreal Canadiens 4 games to 0 to win the Stanley Cup. Boxing: Rocky Marciano knocked out Jersey Joe Walcott in the 13th round to win the World Heavyweight Championship in Philadelphia.

1953

BIRTHS: Cyndi Lauper (June 22) is a pop singer whose first album, 1983's *She's So Unusual,* was the first album in history to have four top 5 singles by a female artist. Ken Burns (July 29) directs and produces documentary films about American culture and history, including *The Civil War, Baseball, Jazz,* and *Prohibition.* Retired professional wrestler Hulk Hogan (August 11) is a 12-time World Heavyweight Champion and the second-longest reigning WWF Champion of all time (behind Bruno Sammartino). Actor John Malkovich (December 9) has starred in such films as *Empire of the Sun, The Killing Fields,* and *Of Mice and Men.* He also created his own fashion label, Technobohemian, in 2011.

ART: William de Kooning completed the abstract expressionist painting *Woman III.* It was displayed at the Tehran Museum of Contemporary Art in Iran until the revolution of 1979, when it was taken down due to strict rules about visual arts imposed by the new government. In 2006, it became the 3rd most expensive painting ever sold, at $137.5 million, by record executive David Geffen to billionaire Steven A. Cohen.

FILM & TV: *From Here to Eternity* starring Burt Lancaster and Deborah Kerr won the Best Picture Academy Award. Other top films were *The Robe* starring Richard Burton and Jean Simmons; *Shane* starring Alan Ladd; *Gentlemen Prefer Blondes* starring Marilyn Monroe; and *Roman Holiday* starring Gregory Peck and Audrey Hepburn. The Disney animated film version of *Peter Pan* was the top grossing movie of 1953, earning over $87 million. Steve McQueen and John Cassavetes made their film debuts. On January 19, 68% of all TV sets in the U.S. were tuned in to watch Lucille Ball give birth to her son little Ricky on *I Love Lucy.* Desi Arnaz and Lucille Ball signed an $8 million contract to continue the *I Love Lucy* TV series through 1955.

INDUSTRY: Banquet Foods started with their line of frozen meat pies. Denny's family restaurant chain was founded in Lakewood, California. The Sonic Drive-In fast food restaurant chain was founded in Shawnee, Oklahoma. Baskin-Robbins chain of ice cream parlors opened in Glendale, California. Jack Odell invented the first Matchbox toy car for his daughter.

LITERATURE: Works published include Ray Bradbury's *Fahrenheit 451;* William S. Burroughs' *Junkie;* Raymond Chandler's *The Long Goodbye;* and Davis Grubb's *The Night of the Hunter.* The iconic character James Bond was first introduced in Ian Fleming's novel, *Casino Royale.*

MUSIC: Popular songs included Les Paul and Mary Ford's "Vaya Con Dios;" Tony Bennett's "Rags to Riches;" Dean Martin's "That's Amore;" Patti Page's "The Doggie in the Window;" Hank Williams' "Your Cheatin' Heart;" and Perry Como's "Don't Let the Stars Get in Your Eyes."

SPORTS: Baseball: The AL's New York Yankees defeated the NL's Brooklyn Dodgers 4 games to 2 in the World Series. Football: The Detroit Lions beat the Cleveland Browns 17-16 to win the NFL Championship. The University of Maryland Terrapins were college football national champions with a 10-1 record. Basketball: The Minneapolis Lakers defeated the New York Knicks 4 games to 1 in the NBA Finals.

THEATRE: The Tony Award for Outstanding Play went to Arthur Miller's *The Crucible* and the Tony Award for Outstanding Musical went to Leonard Bernstein's *Wonderful Town.*

1954

BIRTHS: Photographer Cindy Sherman (January 19) is best known for her conceptual portraits that are among the most expensive photographs ever sold, including her *Untitled #96,* that went for just under $4 million in 2011. Oprah Winfrey (January 29) hosted the #1 TV talk show from 1986 to 2011 and is considered by many to be the most influential woman in the world. Matt Groening (February 15) is the creator of the animated TV series *The Simpsons,* which at over 500 episodes and 23 seasons is the longest-running primetime program in American history. Blues guitarist Stevie Ray Vaughan (October 3) was ranked #12 in *Rolling Stone* magazine's list of '100 Greatest Guitarists' in 2011.

ART & ARCHITECTURE: Norman Rockwell painted one of his masterpieces, *Breaking Home Ties,* for the cover of the September 25 cover of *The Saturday Evening Post* magazine. Sculptor Frank Vittor created the statue of baseball great Honus Wagner, which stands outside PNC Park, the home stadium of Major League Baseball's Pittsburgh Pirates.

FILM & TV: *On the Waterfront* won the Best Picture Academy Award as well as the Best Director Oscar for Elia Kazan, the Best Actor Oscar for Marlon Brando, and the Best Supporting Actress Oscar for Eva Marie Saint. Other top films were *Rear Window* starring James Stewart and Grace Kelly; *White Christmas* starring Bing Crosby, Danny Kaye, and Rosemary Clooney; *20,000 Leagues Under the Sea* starring Kirk Douglas, James Mason, and Peter Lorre; *The Caine Mutiny* starring Humphrey Bogart and Fred MacMurray; and *The Country Girl,* for which Grace Kelly won the Best Actress Academy Award. Paul Newman, Jack Lemmon, Omar Sharif, and Godzilla made their film debuts. TV show premieres included *Lassie, The Wonderful World of Disney, Father Knows Best,* and *The Tonight Show.*

INDUSTRY: The first Swanson TV Dinner cost 98 cents and consisted of turkey, mashed potatoes, cornbread dressing, and buttered peas. Swanson sold more than 10 million of these dinners in its first year of production. Nash Motors merged with the Hudson Motor Car Company to form American Motors. Texas Instruments introduced the Regency TR-1, the world's first transistor radio. The Burger King fast food restaurant chain was founded in Miami, Florida. The first Putt-Putt miniature golf course opened in Fayetteville, North Carolina and cost 25 cents per game.

MUSIC: Popular songs included Kitty Kallen's "Little Things Mean a Lot;" The Chordettes' "Mr. Sandman;" Rosemary Clooney's "Hey There;" The Crew Cuts' "Sh-Boom;" Doris Day's "Secret Love;" Perry Como's "Wanted;" Eddie Fisher's "Oh! My Pa-Pa;" and Big Joe Turner's "Shake, Rattle and Roll."

SPORTS: Baseball: The NL's New York Giants swept the AL's Cleveland Indians 4 games to 0 in the World Series. Football: The Cleveland Browns beat the Detroit Lions 56-10 to win the NFL Championship. The Ohio State University Buckeyes were college football national champions with a 9-0 record. Hockey: The Detroit Red Wings defeated the Montreal Canadiens 4 games to 3 to win the NHL's Stanley Cup. Golfer Arnold Palmer won the U.S. Amateur Golf Championship at the Country Club of Detroit.

THEATRE: Mary Martin won the Best Actress Tony Award and Cyril Ritchard the Best Actor Tony Award for the Broadway musical version of *Peter Pan.*

1955

BIRTHS: Eddie Van Halen (January 26) is the guitarist, songwriter, keyboardist, and producer for the hard rock band Van Halen. He is ranked number 8 on *Rolling Stone* magazine's 2011 list of the '100 Greatest Guitarists.' Steve Jobs (February 24) was the co-founder, chairman, and chief executive officer of the consumer electronics company, Apple, Inc. In 2010, *Forbes* magazine estimated his net worth at $8.3 billion. Actor Bruce Willis (March 19) has starred in such Hollywood hit movies as the *Die Hard* series, *Pulp Fiction, the Sixth Sense, Armageddon,* and *Sin City.* Comedienne and actress Whoopi Goldberg (November 13) is one of only 11 people to have won all 4 major American entertainment awards: an Oscar, an Emmy, a Grammy, and a Tony.

FILM & TV: *Marty* won the Best Picture Academy Award as well as the Best Director Oscar for Delbert Mann and the Best Actor Oscar for Ernest Borgnine. Other top films were *Mister Roberts* starring Henry Fonda and James Cagney; *Guys and Dolls* starring Marlon Brando, Jean Simmons, and Frank Sinatra; *Rebel Without a Cause* starring James Dean and Natalie Wood; *The Seven Year Itch* starring Marilyn Monroe and Tom Ewell; *Picnic* starring William Holden and Kim Novak; and *Oklahoma!* starring Gordon MacRae and Shirley Jones. Clint Eastwood, Shirley MacLaine, Dennis Hopper, Elizabeth Montgomery, Walter Matthau, and Angie Dickinson made their film debuts.

TV show premieres included *The Honeymooners, Gunsmoke, The Mickey Mouse Club, Alfred Hitchcock Presents, Captain Kangaroo,* and *The Lawrence Welk Show.* Elvis Presley appeared on TV for the first time, on the country music show *Louisiana Hayride* in Shreveport, Louisiana.

INDUSTRY: The opening of Disneyland in Anaheim, California July 17 was broadcast live on ABC TV. Ray Kroc opened the first McDonald's hamburger franchise in Des Plaines, Illinois.

MUSIC: Popular songs included Bill Haley's "Rock Around the Clock;" Chuck Berry's "Maybelline;" Frank Sinatra's "Love & Marriage;" The McGuire Sisters' "Sincerely;" Little Richard's "Tutti Frutti;" The Penguins' "Earth Angel;" Fats Domino's "Ain't That a Shame;" and Johnny Cash's "Folsom Prison Blues."

SPORTS: Baseball: The NL's Brooklyn Dodgers defeated the AL's New York Yankees 4 games to 3 in the World Series. Football: The Cleveland Browns beat the Los Angeles Rams 38-14 to win the NFL Championship. The University of Oklahoma Sooners were college football national champions with a 10-0 record. Ohio State halfback Howard 'Hopalong' Cassady won the Heisman Trophy. Basketball: The Syracuse Nationals defeated the Fort Wayne Pistons 4 games to 3 to win the NBA Title. Hockey: The Detroit Red Wings beat the Montreal Canadiens 4 games to 3 to win the Stanley Cup. Drag Racing: The National Hot Rod Association (NHRA) staged its first 'Nationals' in Great Bend, Kansas. Calvin Rice won the inaugural 'Top Fuel' Championship.

THEATRE: Tennessee Williams' Pulitzer Prize winning play *Cat on a Hot Tin Roof* opened on Broadway, directed by Elia Kazan and starring Barbara Bel Geddes, Ben Gazzara, and Burl Ives. Other productions included the musical *Damn Yankees* and the plays *Bus Stop* and *Inherit the Wind.*

1956

BIRTHS: Anthony Bourdain (June 25) is a chef, author, and TV host of the Travel Channel's culinary and adventure program, *No Reservations.* Fashion model Jerry Hall (July 2) earned modeling fees of $1,000 a day in the late 1970s and has 4 children with Rolling Stones singer Mick Jagger. Actress Bo Derek (November 20) is best known for the 1979 film *10,* which created a popular cornrow hairstyle in the early 1980s and made her an international sex symbol. Larry Bird (December 7) is a former professional basketball player, coach, and team president. He starred in 13 seasons for the Boston Celtics, where he won 3 NBA Championship Titles and 3 NBA Most Valuable Player Awards.

ARCHITECTURE: Resembling a stack of records on a turntable, the 13-story tall Capitol Records Building in Hollywood, California was designed by architect Welton Becket and is the world's first round office building. The blinking light at the top of the tower's antenna spire spells out the word 'Hollywood' in Morse code and was first switched on by Leila Morse, the granddaughter of Samuel Morse.

FILM & TV: *Around the World in Eighty Days* won the Best Picture Academy Award. Other top films were *The Ten Commandments,* directed by Cecil B. DeMille and starring Charlton Heston and Yul Brynner; *Giant* starring Rock Hudson, Elizabeth Taylor, and James Dean; *War and Peace* starring Audrey Hepburn and Henry Fonda; *The King and I* starring Yul Brynner and Deborah Kerr; *Bus Stop* starring Marilyn Monroe and Don Murray; and *The Searchers,* directed by John Ford and starring John Wayne. Elvis Presley, James Garner, Leslie Nielsen, and Rip Torn made their film debuts. TV show premieres included *The Steve Allen Show; Playhouse 90; The Price Is Right; My Friend Flicka; As the World Turns; The Edge of Night;* and *Queen for a Day.* Elvis Presley was paid $50,000 to appear on 3 Ed Sullivan shows.

INDUSTRY: Play-Doh, the modeling compound used by children for art and craft projects, was first used as a wallpaper cleaner. The inventor's nephew noticed schoolchildren making Christmas ornaments from Play-Doh and began marketing it as a toy for children. The dice game Yahtzee has remained popular since its creation, selling 50 million games annually.

MUSIC: Elvis Presley had the top 3 singles of 1956: "Hound Dog," "Heartbreak Hotel," and "Don't Be Cruel." Other popular songs included Fats Domino's "Blueberry Hill;" The Platters' "The Great Pretender;" Carl Perkins' "Blue Suede Shoes;" Gene Vincent's "Be-Bop-A-Lula;" Dean Martin's "Memories Are Made of This;" and Guy Mitchell's "Singing the Blues."

SPORTS: Baseball: The AL's New York Yankees defeated the NL's Brooklyn Dodgers 4 games to 3 in the World Series. Yankees pitcher Don Larsen pitched the only perfect game in World Series history, earning MVP honors. Pittsburgh Pirates outfielder Roberto Clemente became the only player in MLB history to hit a walk-off inside-the-park grand slam home run, against the Chicago Cubs July 25 at Pittsburgh's Forbes Field. Football: The New York Giants beat the Chicago Bears 47-7 to win the NFL Championship. The University of Oklahoma Sooners were college football national champions with a 10-0 record.

THEATRE: Eugene O'Neill's play *Long Day's Journey Into Night* won the Pulitzer Prize fro Drama and the Tony Award for Best Play.

1957

BIRTHS: Pro golfer Nancy Lopez (January 6) has 52 tournament victories and is the only woman to win the LPGA Rookie of the Year, Player of the Year, and the Vare Trophy (lowest scoring average) in the same year (1978). Katie Couric (January 7) is a journalist who hosted NBC's morning TV news/talk program, *The Today Show* from 1991 to 2006. Spike Lee (March 20) has produced, directed, written, and starred in such films as *Do the Right Thing, Mo' Better Blues, Jungle Fever,* and *Malcolm X.* Singer and former teen idol Donny Osmond (December 9) started his performing career with his 4 elder brothers as The Osmonds, then teamed with his sister Marie on the 1970s hit TV variety show, *Donny & Marie.*

ART: The 'readymade' work *Object to Be Destroyed,* created by artist Man Ray in 1923, was destroyed by a group of protesting students in a gallery in Paris, France, where it was on display. The piece consisted of a metronome with a photograph of an eye attached to its swinging arm. It was destroyed by one of the students who shot it with a pistol.

FILM & TV: *The Bridge on the River Kwai* won the Best Picture Academy Award, as well as the Best Director Oscar for David Lean and the Best Actor Oscar for Alec Guinness. Other top films were *Peyton Place* starring Lana Turner; *Sayonara* starring Marlon Brando and Red Buttons; *Raintree County* starring Montgomery Clift and Elizabeth Taylor; *Gunfight at the O.K. Corral* starring Kirk Douglas and Burt Lancaster; *Island in the Sun* starring James Mason and Joan Fontaine; *Pal Joey* starring Rita Hayworth, Frank Sinatra, and Kim Novak; and *Jailhouse Rock* starring Elvis Presley. Sean Connery, Robert Loggia, and Andy Griffith made their film debuts. TV show premieres included *Leave It To Beaver, Wagon Train, Perry Mason,* and *Maverick.*

INDUSTRY: The Wham-O toy company founders Richard Knerr and Arthur 'Spud' Melin created the Hula Hoop after hearing about Australian schoolchildren twirling bamboo hoops around their waists for exercise in gym class. Wham-O also modified the 'Pluto Platter' plastic flying disc and renamed it the Frisbee.

LITERATURE: Jack Kerouac's autobiographical novel about his spontaneous cross-country travel adventures, *On the Road,* was published. It is considered the defining work of the post-World War II Beat Generation. Dr. Seuss published his children's book classics *The Cat in the Hat* and *How the Grinch Stole Christmas!*

MUSIC: Popular songs included Elvis Presley's "Jailhouse Rock," "All Shook Up," and "Teddy Bear;" Paul Anka's "Diana;" Sam Cooke's "You Send Me;" Jerry Lee Lewis' "Great Balls of Fire;" Buddy Holly's' "That'll Be the Day," "Peggy Sue," "Oh Boy," and "Not Fade Away;" Danny and the Juniors' "At the Hop;" Patsy Cline's "Walkin' After Midnight;" The Everly Brothers' "Wake Up Little Susie" and "Bye, Bye Love;" and Johnny Mathis' "Chances Are."

SPORTS: Baseball: The NL's Milwaukee Brewers defeated the AL's New York Yankees 4 games to 3 in the World Series. On October 8, Brooklyn Dodgers owner Walter O'Malley announced that the team would move to Los Angeles, California. Football: The Detroit Lions beat the Cleveland Browns 59-14 to win the NFL Championship. The Auburn University Tigers were college football national champions with a 10-0 record. Basketball: The Boston Celtics defeated the St. Louis Hawks 4 games to 3 to win the NBA Title.

1958

BIRTHS: Ellen DeGeneres (January 26) has won 13 Emmy Awards as a comedienne and TV talk show host and is the only person to win a Saturn Award for a voice performance, as Dory in the 2003 Disney animated film *Finding Nemo.* Artist Keith Haring (May 4) first gained attention for his chalk drawings in the New York City subways and later designed the album cover for *A Very Special Christmas*. King of Pop Michael Jackson (August 29) had 13 number one singles during his solo career and has sold more than 750 million albums worldwide including the best selling album of all time, 1982's *Thriller,* which has sold over 100 million copies. Actress Jamie Lee Curtis (November 22) is the daughter of actors Tony Curtis and Janet Leigh and is married to actor Christopher Guest.

ARCHITECTURE: Standing 516 feet tall with 38 stories, the Seagram Building in New York City is a masterpiece of modern architecture. Designed by Ludwig Mies van der Rohe, the building used 1,500 tons of bronze in its construction. The Time-Life Building in New York City's Rockefeller Center was designed by Wallace Harrison and stands 587 feet tall with 48 floors.

FILM & TV: *Gigi* won the Best Picture Academy Award and the Best Director Oscar for Vincente Minnelli. Other top films were *South Pacific* starring Mitzi Gaynor; *Cat on a Hot Tin Roof* starring Paul Newman and Elizabeth Taylor; *Auntie Mamie* starring Rosalind Russell; *The Vikings* starring Kirk Douglas, Tony Curtis, and Janet Leigh; *No Time for Sergeants* starring Andy Griffith; and *Vertigo* starring James Stewart and Kim Novak. Jack Nicholson, Suzanne Pleshette, Christopher Plummer, Maggie Smith, Oliver Reed, and Vanessa Redgrave made their film debuts. TV show premieres included *Sea Hunt, The Rifleman, Concentration,* and *The Huckleberry Hound Show.*

INDUSTRY: The Ford Motor Company introduced the Edsel automobile, which sold miserably and lost Ford $350 million during its 3 years of production. With less than 10,000 Edsels surviving today, they are valuable collector's items sometimes selling for over $100,000. Bank of America launched the *BankAmericard,* the first modern credit card, which later evolved into the Visa card system. The restaurant chains Pizza Hut, IHOP (formerly known as The International House of Pancakes), Perkins, and Sizzler all started in 1958.

MUSIC: Popular songs included The Kingston Trio's "Tom Dooley;" Eddie Cochran's "Summertime Blues;" Tommy Edwards' "It's All in the Game;" The Everly Brothers' "All I Have To Do Is Dream" and "Bird Dog;" Conway Twitty's "It's Only Make Believe;" The Platters' "Smoke Gets in Your Eyes;" Ricky Nelson's "Poor Little Fool;" Connie Francis' "Who's Sorry Now?;" Chuck Berry's "Sweet Little Sixteen;" The Coasters' "Yakety Yak;" Peggy Lee's "Fever;" and Don Gibson's "Oh, Lonesome Me."

SPORTS: Baseball: The AL's New York Yankees defeated the NL's Milwaukee Braves 4 games to 3 in the World Series. Football: In the 'Greatest Game Ever Played,' the Baltimore Colts beat the New York Giants 23-17 in overtime to win the NFL Championship. The Louisiana State University Tigers won their first college football national championship with an 11-0 record. Basketball: The St. Louis Hawks defeated the Boston Celtics 4 games to 2 to win the NBA Title. Golf: Arnold Palmer won the Masters Tournament and was the PGA money leader, earning $42,608 for the season.

1959

BIRTHS: John McEnroe (February 16) is a former professional tennis player with 104 career tournament titles including 4 U.S. Open and 3 Wimbledon championships. He posted the best ever single season tennis win-loss record in 1984 at 82-3. Emeril Lagasse (October 15) is a celebrity chef, restaurateur, and cookbook author whose ventures generate $150 million in revenue annually. Musician Weird Al Yankovic (October 23) has recorded hit parody songs of Michael Jackson's "Beat It ("Eat It"), Queen's "Another One Bites the Dust" ("Another One Rides the Bus"), and Madonna's "Like a Virgin" (Like a Surgeon"). Sprinter Florence Griffith-Joyner (December 21) won 4 Olympic gold medals and 3 silver medals during her career. Flo-Jo is considered the 'fastest woman of all time' based on the world records she set in 1988 for both the 100 and 200 meters; records that still stand today.

ARCHITECTURE: Designed by Frank Lloyd Wright, the Solomon R. Guggenheim Museum in New York City is a cylindrical shaped building that is wider at the top than the bottom. The Bailey House and Stahl House, both designed by Pierre Koenig and built in Los Angeles, California, were part of the Case Study Houses Program sponsored by *Arts & Architecture* magazine during the mid 1900s. Stahl House was included in a 2008 *Los Angeles Times* newspaper list of the all-time top 10 houses in Los Angeles.

FILM & TV: *Ben-Hur* won the Best Picture Academy Award as well as the Best Director Oscar for William Wyler, the Best Actor Oscar for Charlton Heston, and the Best Supporting Actor Oscar for Hugh Griffith. Other top films were *North by Northwest* starring Cary Grant and Eva Marie Saint; *Some Like It Hot* starring Marilyn Monroe, Tony Curtis, and Jack Lemmon; *Pillow Talk* starring Doris Day and Rock Hudson; *Suddenly, Last Summer* starring Elizabeth Taylor, Montgomery Clift, and Katherine Hepburn; *Imitation of Life* starring Lana Turner; and *Rio Bravo* starring John Wayne and Dean Martin. TV show premieres included *Rawhide, The Twilight Zone,* and *Bonanza* (the first weekly TV series broadcast completely in color).

INDUSTRY: Inspired by a German doll called Bild Lilli, businesswoman Ruth Handler created the iconic Barbie Doll. Mattel has sold more than 800 million Barbie Dolls worldwide. Berry Gordy Jr. founded Motown Records with $800 that he borrowed from his family.

LITERATURE: Published works include William S. Burroughs' *Naked Lunch;* Richard Condon's *The Manchurian Candidate;* James Michener's *Hawaii;* Kurt Vonnegut's *The Sirens of Titan;* and Allen Drury's Pulitzer Prize winning novel, *Advise and Consent.*

MUSIC: Domenico Modugno's "Volare" won the first Song of the Year Grammy Award. Other top songs were Bobby Darin's "Mack the Knife" and "Beyond the Sea;" Marty Robbins' "El Paso;" Lloyd Price's "Personality;" and Ray Charles' "What'd I Say." Buddy Holly, Ritchie Valens, and The Big Bopper were killed in a plane crash near Clear Lake, Iowa on 'The Day the Music Died,' February 3.

SPORTS: Baseball: The NL's Los Angeles Dodgers defeated the AL's Chicago White Sox 4 games to 2 in the World Series. Football: The Baltimore Colts beat the New York Giants 31-16 to win the NFL Championship. Motor Racing: Lee Petty won the inaugural Daytona 500 in a photo finish.

THEATRE: The Rodgers and Hammerstein musical *The Sound of Music* starred Mary Martin as Maria and ran for 1,443 Broadway performances.

1960

On April 1, the U.S. population was 179,323,175 people. The average yearly income for a U.S. worker was $4,007, equal to $29,600 today; the average house cost $20,556, equal to $151,847 today; the average car cost $2,600, equal to $19,206 today; a gallon of gas cost 31 cents, equal to $2.29 today; and a pack of chewing gum cost 5 cents, equal to 37 cents today.

BIRTHS: John Elway (June 28) played quarterback for the National Football League's Denver Broncos from 1983 to 1998. He led the Broncos to 2 Super Bowl Titles and was the NFL's Most Valuable Player in 1987. Jazz saxophonist Branford Marsalis (August 26) led the Tonight Show Band on *The Tonight Show with Jay Leno* from 1992 to 1995. John F. Kennedy, Jr. (November 25) founded *George* magazine in 1995 but died 4 years later when the small airplane he was piloting crashed into the Atlantic Ocean. Fashion model Carol Alt (December 1) gained fame in 1982 when she was featured on the cover of *Sports Illustrated* magazine's swimsuit issue and appeared on over 500 magazine covers during the 1980s.

FILM & TV: *The Apartment* won the Best Picture Academy Award. Other top films were *Psycho; Swiss Family Robinson; Spartacus;* and *Exodus.* Marilyn Monroe and Clark Gable starred in *The Misfits*, the last film either performed in. John F. Kennedy and Richard Nixon appeared in the first presidential debate to be broadcast on TV. *The Andy Griffith Show; Route 66; The Flintstones; My Three Sons;* and *The Bugs Bunny Show* made their TV debuts in 1960.

INDUSTRY: Domino's Pizza was founded in Detroit, Michigan. The Chevrolet Corvair was the first American car to have a rear engine and was chosen as *Motor Trend* magazine's 'Car of the Year.' Kazuo Hashimoto invented the Ansafone, sold in the U.S. as the first automatic telephone-answering machine. NASA launched the first weather satellite, TIROS-1, from Cape Canaveral, Florida. Chatty Cathy, the first talking doll, spoke 11 random phrases at the pull of a string. The original voice was June Foray, who also voiced Rocket J. Squirrel in the Rocky and Bullwinkle cartoons. The classic toys Etch-a-Sketch and Legos were also introduced to American consumers.

MUSIC: Johnny Horton's "The Battle of New Orleans" won the Song of the Year Grammy Award. Bobby Darin won Best New Artist. Other top songs were Elvis Presley's "It's Now or Never" and "Are You Lonesome Tonight," Chubby Checker's "The Twist," and The Drifters' "Save the Last Dance For Me."

SPORTS: Baseball: The NL's Pittsburgh Pirates defeated the AL's New York Yankees 4 games to 3 in the World Series. Pittsburgh's Bill Mazeroski became the first player to hit a game-winning home run in the 7th game to win a World Series. Football: The Philadelphia Eagles beat the Green Bay Packers 17-13 to win the NFL Championship. The American Football League played its first season with the Houston Oilers defeating the Los Angeles Chargers 24-16 in the AFL Championship. The United States Olympic men's ice hockey team won its first Olympic hockey gold medal with a record of 7-0-0. The largest crash in NASCAR history happened at the Daytona 500 when 37 of the 68 cars that started the race got into a massive wreck.

THEATRE: The Tony Award winning Broadway musical *Bye Bye Birdie* starred Dick Van Dyke, Paul Lynde, and Charles Nelson Riley.

1961

BIRTHS: Eddie Murphy (April 3) is a comedian and actor. Box office totals from his films place him second to Samuel L. Jackson as the highest-grossing actor in Hollywood history. Musician Kim Deal (June 10) is best known as the bassist for the alternative rock band the Pixies and the lead vocalist and rhythm guitarist for The Breeders. Track and field athlete Carl Lewis (July 1) won 9 Olympic gold medals and 10 World Championships from 1979 to 1996. His world record in the indoor long jump has stood since 1984. Fashion designer Tom Ford (August 27) first gained fame by reviving Gucci as creative director from 1994 to 2004, before launching his own Tom Ford label in 2005.

ART & ARCHITECTURE: Pop artist Roy Lichtenstein created the paintings *Engagement Ring* and *Look Mickey,* both featuring speech balloons. Seattle's Space Needle was built for the 1962 World's Fair and was the tallest structure west of the Mississippi River. The Pittsburgh Civic Arena was the world's first retractable roof sports venue.

FILM & TV: *West Side Story* won the Best Picture Academy Award plus nine more Oscars. Other top films were *El Cid, The Guns of Navarone, Breakfast at Tiffany's* and *Blue Hawaii.* Gene Hackman, Burt Reynolds, Warren Beatty, And Louis Gossett, Jr. made their film debuts. John F. Kennedy held the first live televised Presidential press conference on January 25. The launch of the Freedom 7 spacecraft carrying Alan Shepard, the first U.S. astronaut in space, was watched by 45 million TV viewers on May 5. *The Dick Van Dyke Show; ABC's Wide World of Sports; Mr. Ed; Car 54 Where Are You?; Hazel;* and *The Mike Douglas Show* debuted on TV in 1961.

INDUSTRY: Frito-Lay was formed in Plano, Texas and has grown into the largest globally distributed snack food company in the world. Six Flags Entertainment Corp. has become the world's largest amusement park corporation with 14 properties throughout North America. The 1961 Lincoln Continental featured front-opening rear 'suicide doors' and was the first American car to come with a full 24,000 mile or 2-year warranty. Sony introduced the first videotape recorder. General Electric produced the first rechargeable cordless toothbrush. Barbie's boyfriend, the Ken doll, and the Duncan Yo-Yo were also introduced.

MUSIC: Ernest Gold's "Theme of *Exodus"* won the Song of the Year Grammy Award. Bob Newhart won Best New Artist. Other top songs were Ben E. King's "Stand By Me;" Del Shannon's "Runaway;" Chubby Checker's "Let's Twist Again;" and Elvis Presley's "Surrender." The Beach Boys released their first single, "Surfin".

SPORTS: Baseball: The AL's New York Yankees defeated the NL's Cincinnati Reds 4 games to 1 in the World Series. Yankees outfielder Roger Maris hit 61 home runs to break Babe Ruth's single season record. The Yankees' Mickey Mantle became the highest paid player at $75,000 per season. Football: Minnesota Vikings quarterback Fran Tarkenton came off the bench in his pro debut and led the Vikings to an upset win over the Chicago Bears in the team's first game. Hockey: The Chicago Blackhawks beat the Detroit Red Wings 4 games to 2, to win the Stanley Cup.

1962

BIRTHS: Musician Jon Bon Jovi (March 2) is the lead singer of the rock band Bon Jovi and has sold over 130 million albums worldwide. Billy Beane (March 29) is the general manager of Major League Baseball's Oakland A's. Beane's new approach to evaluating talent was the subject of *Moneyball,* a 2003 book by author Michael Lewis and 2011 film starring Brad Pitt as Beane. Paula Abdul (June 19) was a cheerleader for the Los Angeles Lakers and choreographed music videos before charting 6 number one singles as a pop singer in the late 1980s. She served as a judge on TV's *American Idol* for 8 seasons until 2009. Bo Jackson (November 30) became the first professional athlete to be named an All Star in 2 major American sports: for Major League Baseball's Kansas City Royals in 1989 and the NFL's Los Angeles Raiders in 1990.

ART & ARCHITECTURE: Stan Lee and Jack Kirby created the comic book character *The Incredible Hulk*. Stan Lee also created the comic book character *Spider-Man,* with Steve Ditko. Andy Warhol's first one-man gallery opened in Los Angeles, California featuring his pop art piece *Campbell's Soup Cans.* The Minolta Tower opened in Niagara Falls, Ontario, Canada. It was the first observation tower built near the brink of the falls.

FILM & TV: *Lawrence of Arabia* won the Best Picture Academy Award. Other top films were *Dr. No* (which launched the James Bond film series, the longest continually-running film franchise in history); *The Longest Day; How the West Was Won;* and *Mutiny on the Bounty.* Robert Duvall, Sally Field, Sydney Pollack, and John Schlesinger made their film debuts. The Rose Bowl was the first coast-to-coast color TV broadcast of a college football game in the U.S., with the Minnesota Golden Gophers beating the UCLA Bruins 21-3. Walter Cronkite succeeded Douglas Edwards as anchorman of the *CBS Evening News,* a job he held until 1981. *The Lucy Show; The Tonight Show Starring Johnny Carson; McHale's Navy; The Beverly Hillbillies; The Virginian;* and *The Jetsons* debuted on TV in 1962.

INDUSTRY: The largest retailer in the world, Walmart, was founded in Bentonville, Arkansas. The first American car to use a V6 engine, the Buick Special, was *Motor Trend* magazine's 'Car of the Year.' Diet Rite and Tab were introduced as the first sugarless soft drink colas. Nick Holonyak of General Electric invented the LED (Light Emitting Diode).

MUSIC: Henry Mancini's "Moon River" won the Song of the Year Grammy Award. Peter Nero won Best New Artist. Other top songs were Elvis Presley's "Return to Sender" and "Can't Help Falling in Love," Ray Charles' "I Can't Stop Loving You," and The Tornados "Telstar" (the first song by a British group to reach number one on the Billboard Top 100 Charts, starting the 'British Invasion'). Herb Alpert and Jerry Moss founded A&M Records.

SPORTS: Baseball: The AL's New York Yankees beat the NL's San Francisco Giants 4 games to 3 in the World Series. Football: The Green Bay Packers won 16-7 over the New York Giants in the NFL Championship. The Dallas Texans defeated the Houston Oilers 20-17 in double overtime in the AFL Championship. The Philadelphia Warriors' Wilt Chamberlain set the National Basketball Association single game scoring record when he scored 100 points against the New York Knicks on March 2 in Hershey, Pennsylvania.

1963

BIRTHS: Michael Jordan (February 17) was named North America's greatest athlete of the 20th century by ESPN in 1999. During his professional basketball-playing career he won 6 NBA Championships and 6 NBA Finals Most Valuable Player awards. Rick Rubin (March 10) helped popularize hip-hop music by producing albums by the Beastie Boys, Run-D.M.C., and LL Cool J, among others. Fashion designer Marc Jacobs (April 9) is the head designer for his own brand as well as the creative director of the Louis Vuitton fashion house. Actor Johnny Depp (June 9) is best known for playing Captain Jack Sparrow in the *Pirates of the Caribbean* film series. He is listed by *Forbes* magazine as the world's highest paid actor with 2012 earnings of $75 million.

ART & ARCHITECTURE: Andy Warhol produced the silkscreen painting, *Eight Elvises,* which was reportedly sold to a private collector in 2009 for $100 million. The Morris Louis memorial exhibition celebrated his Color Field paintings at the Guggenheim Museum in New York City. When the MetLife Building opened in New York City as the Pan Am Building, it contained the largest commercial office space in the world.

FILM & TV: *Tom Jones* won the Best Picture Academy Award. Other top films were *Cleopatra; It's a Mad, Mad, Mad, Mad World; The Birds;* and *From Russia with Love.* Actor Steve McQueen performed his own motorcycle stunts in the World War II epic film *The Great Escape.* Alan Alda, James Caan, Kurt Russell, Alan Arkin, and Tippi Hedren, made their film debuts. Instant Replay was used on TV for the first time during the Army Navy college football game. On November 22, CBS TV's Walter Cronkite interrupted the live soap opera *As the World Turns* to announce the news of President John F. Kennedy's assassination. Two days later Jack Ruby shot and killed JFK's suspected assassin Lee Harvey Oswald on live television. *The Fugitive; Petticoat Junction; The Patty Duke Show; General Hospital; The Outer Limits;* and *Mutual of Omaha's Wild Kingdom* debuted on TV in 1963.

INDUSTRY: AT&T began selling touch-tone telephones to consumers; early models had only 10 buttons, the 'star' and 'pound' keys were added in 1968. Commercial artist Harvey Ball created the yellow 'Smiley Face' symbol but never applied for a trademark or copyright and earned just $45 for his work. Kenner introduced the Easy Bake Oven, America's first working toy oven, which sold 500,000 units in its first year at a hefty price of $15.95.

MUSIC: Anthony Newley's "What Kind of Fool Am I?" won the Song of the Year Grammy Award. Robert Goulet won Best New Artist. Other top songs were The Beatles' "She Loves You," The Kingsmen's "Louie Louie," Paul and Paula's "Hey Paula," and Lesley Gore's "It's My Party." Bob Dylan walked off *The Ed Sullivan Show* when told he could not perform his anti-segregationist song, "Talking John Birch Society Blues." Country music star Patsy Cline was killed in a small plane crash near Camden, Tennessee.

SPORTS: Baseball: The NL's Los Angeles Dodgers swept the AL's New York Yankees 4 games to 0 in the World Series. Football: The San Diego Chargers beat the Boston Patriots 51-10 to win the AFL Championship. The Chicago Bears won the NFL Championship 14-10 over the New York Giants. The Pro Football Hall of Fame opened in Canton, Ohio with 17 charter members including Sammy Baugh, Harold 'Red' Grange, Bronco Nagurski, George Halas, Earl 'Curly' Lambeau, Don Hutson, and Jim Thorpe.

1964

BIRTHS: Laird Hamilton (March 2) is a big-wave surfer and the inventor of tow-in surfing. He is credited with surfing the 'heaviest wave ever ridden' at Teahupo'o, Tahiti, on August 17, 2000, documented in the film *Riding Giants.* Musician Lenny Kravitz (May 26) is a 4-time Grammy Award winner and a multi-instrumentalist incorporating rock, R&B, reggae, and funk styles. Joss Whedon (June 23) created the TV series *Buffy the Vampire Slayer* in 1997 and wrote and directed the 2012 film adaptation of Marvel Comics' *The Avengers,* the third highest-grossing film of all time. Celebrity chef Bobby Flay (December 10) is the owner and executive chef of 12 restaurants and has hosted 7 TV cooking shows on the Food Network.

ART & ARCHITECTURE: Norman Rockwell painted *The Problem We All Live With,* which depicts an African-American girl on her way to an all-white public school during 1960s racial segregation. Andy Warhol produced the *Shot Marilyns,* a pop art piece featuring 4 square images of Marilyn Monroe shot through the forehead. The 52-story Prudential Tower became the second-tallest building in Boston, Massachusetts. The Los Angeles County Museum of Art opened with a collection of over 100,000 works.

FILM & TV: *My Fair Lady* won the Best Picture Academy Award as well as the Best Director Oscar for George Cukor and the Best Actor Oscar for Rex Harrison. Other top movies were *Mary Poppins* starring Julie Andrews (Best Actress Oscar winner) and Dick Van Dyke; *Goldfinger* and *From Russia With Love* starring Sean Connery; *The Pink Panther* and *A Shot in the Dark* starring Peter Sellers; *The Carpetbaggers* starring George Peppard; *Hush...Hush, Sweet Charlotte* starring Bette Davis; *Viva Las Vegas* starring Elvis Presley and Ann-Margret; and the first Beatles film, *A Hard Day's Night.* Donald Sutherland and James Earl Jones made their film debuts. TV show premieres included *Bewitched; The Addams Family; Gilligan's Island; Flipper; The Man from U.N.C.L.E.; Daniel Boone; The Munsters; Gomer Pyle, U.S.M.C.;* and the Christmas special, *Rudolph the Red-Nosed Reindeer.* A record setting 73 million people watched The Beatles' first U.S. television appearance on *The Ed Sullivan Show,* February 9.

INDUSTRY: Nike, the world's largest maker of athletic shoes, was named for the Greek Goddess of victory. The Hasbro Toy Company coined the phrase 'action figure' with its introduction of the 12-inch 'G.I. Joe' figure, representing the 4 branches of the U.S. military: Army (Action Soldier), Navy (Action Sailor), Air Force (Action Pilot), and Marines (Action Marine).

MUSIC: Henry Mancini's "Days of Wine and Roses" won the Song of the Year Grammy Award. Other top songs were The Beatles' "I Want to Hold Your Hand," "I Feel Fine," and "A Hard Day's Night;" Roy Orbison's "Oh, Pretty Woman;" The Supremes' "Baby Love;" The Beach Boys' "I Get Around;" and Martha and the Vandellas' "Dancing in the Street."

SPORTS: Baseball: The NL's St. Louis Cardinals defeated the AL's New York Yankees 4 games to 3 in the World Series. Football: The Cleveland Browns beat the Baltimore Colts 27-0 to win the NFL Championship. The University of Alabama Crimson Tide were college football national champions with a 10-1 record.

THEATRE: The Broadway musical *Hello, Dolly!* starred Carol Channing and won 10 Tony Awards. It ran for 2,844 performances and nearly 7 years.

1965

BIRTHS: Chris Rock (February 7) created and narrated *Everybody Hates Chris,* a TV sitcom about his experiences growing up in Brooklyn, New York. He was voted the 5th greatest stand-up comedian of all time by Comedy Central. Dr. Dre (February 18) is a pioneer artist in rap and hip-hop music, guiding the careers of Snoop Dogg, Eminem, and 50 Cent, among others. Actress Brooke Shields (May 31) began as a model for Ivory Soap at the age of 11 months and was the youngest model ever to appear on the cover of *Vogue* magazine, when she was 14. She starred in the films *Blue Lagoon* (1980) and *Endless Love* (1981). Producer Ryan Murphy (November 9) has created the hit TV shows *Nip/Tuck, Glee,* and *American Horror Story.*

ARCHITECTURE: The stainless steel Gateway Arch in St. Louis, Missouri, is the tallest man-made monument in the U.S. It stands 630 feet tall and 630 feet wide at its base. A unique tram system carries visitors to an observation room at the top of the arch. The Astrodome in Houston, Texas was the world's first multi-purpose, domed sports stadium.

FILM & TV: *The Sound of Music* won the Best Picture Academy Award and the Best Director Oscar for Robert Wise. Other top films were *Cat Ballou* starring Lee Marvin (Best Actor Oscar) and Jane Fonda; *Doctor Zhivago* starring Omar Sharif and Julie Christie; *The Great Race* starring Tony Curtis, Jack Lemmon, and Natalie Wood; *That Darn Cat* starring Hayley Mills and Dean Jones; and *Those Magnificent Men in Their Flying Machines* starring Stuart Whitman and Sarah Miles. Woody Allen and Ed Asner made their film debuts. TV show premieres included *Get Smart; I Dream of Jeannie; F Troop; Hogan's Heroes; I Spy; Green Acres; The Wild Wild West;* and *Lost in Space. A Charlie Brown Christmas* was the first *Peanuts* animated TV special.

INDUSTRY: Ford introduced the iconic Mustang, which created the 'pony car' class of sports cars with long hoods and short rear decks. Milton Bradley introduced 'Operation', the classic battery-operated game that tests players' hand-eye coordination. Mattel's 'See 'n Say' educational toy has helped millions of children learn new vocabulary with its unique dial and pull string.

LITERATURE: Frank Herbert's novel *Dune* is the best selling science fiction novel of all time. Truman Capote spent 6 years writing *In Cold Blood* from the thousands of pages of notes he collected with friend and fellow author Harper Lee about the brutal murders of a Kansas farm family in 1959.

MUSIC: Louis Armstrong's "Hello, Dolly!" won the Song of the Year Grammy Award. The Beatles won Best New Artist. Other top songs were The Righteous Brothers' "You've Lost That Loving Feeling" (the most played song in American radio history), and the top 2 songs on *Rolling Stone* magazine's 2004 list of 'The 500 Greatest Songs of All Time': Bob Dylan's "Like a Rolling Stone" at #1 and The Rolling Stones' "(I Can't Get No) Satisfaction" at #2.

SPORTS: Baseball: The NL's Los Angeles Dodgers defeated the AL's Minnesota Twins 4 games to 3 in the World Series. Football: The Green Bay Packers beat the Cleveland Browns 23-12 to win the NFL Championship. Golf: Gary Player became the 3rd golfer in history to win the 'Grand Slam': all 4 professional majors in one season.

THEATRE: The original production of Neil Simon's Broadway play *The Odd Couple* was directed by Mike Nichols and starred Walter Matthau and Art Carney. The Broadway musical *Fiddler on the Roof* won 9 Tony Awards and was the first musical in history to surpass 3,000 performances (3,242).

1966

BIRTHS: Model Cindy Crawford (February 20) has appeared on over 400 magazine covers and signed multi-million dollar endorsement contracts with Revlon and Pepsi. She was married to actor Richard Gere in the early 1990s. Mike Tyson (June 30) became the youngest boxer in history to win the WBC, WBA, and IBF heavyweight titles at the age of 20. He won his first 19 professional bouts by knockout, 12 of them in the first round. Adam Sandler (September 9) was Hollywood's highest paid actor in the 2000s, earning $25 million per movie and has starred in several films that have each grossed over $100 million at the box office. Adam Horovitz (October 31), better known as his stage name Ad-Rock, became a member of the pioneering hip hop group Beastie Boys in 1982 at the age of 16.

ARCHITECTURE: NASA's Vehicle Assembly Building at the Kennedy Space Center in Titusville, Florida was designed for the vertical assembly of the Saturn V rocket. At 526 feet tall, it is the largest single-story building in the world. The Whitney Museum of American Art in New York City houses a collection of nearly 20,000 modern art pieces by over 2,900 artists.

FILM & TV: *A Man for All Seasons* won the Best Picture Academy Award as well as the Best Director Oscar for Fred Zinnemann and the Best Actor Oscar for Paul Scofield. Other top films were *The Sand Pebbles* starring Steve McQueen and Candice Bergen; *Who's Afraid of Virginia Woolf?* starring Elizabeth Taylor (Best Actress Oscar) and Richard Burton; *Hawaii* starring Julie Andrews and Max von Sydow; and *Grand Prix* starring James Garner and Eva Marie Saint. Harrison Ford, Michael Douglas, and Christopher Walken made their film debuts. TV show premieres included *Star Trek; The Monkees; Dark Shadows; Mission: Impossible; That Girl; Batman;* and the animated special, *How the Grinch Stole Christmas,* narrated by Boris Karloff.

INDUSTRY: The first American car with front wheel drive, the Oldsmobile Toronado, was *Motor Trend* magazine's Car of the Year. The Twister game uses human bodies as playing pieces and became a success when actress Eva Gabor played it with Johnny Carson on *The Tonight Show,* May 3. The Spirograph and Rock 'Em Sock 'Em Robots were also introduced in 1966.

LITERATURE: *Valley of the Dolls,* Jacqueline Susann's first novel, has sold more than 30 million copies. Other published works include Isaac Asimov's *Fantastic Voyage,* Larry McMurtry's *The Last Picture Show,* Daniel Keyes' *Flowers for Algernon,* and Arthur M. Schlesinger, Jr.'s *A Thousand Days.*

MUSIC: Tony Bennett's "The Shadow of Your Smile" won the Song of the Year Grammy Award. Tom Jones won Best New Artist. Other top songs were The Beach Boys' "Good Vibrations," Donavan's "Mellow Yellow," and Percy Sledge's "When a Man Loves a Woman."

SPORTS: Baseball: The AL's Baltimore Orioles swept the NL's Los Angeles Dodgers 4 games to 0 in the World Series. Football: The Green Bay Packers beat the Dallas Cowboys 34-27 to win the NFL Championship. The University of Notre Dame Fighting Irish were college football national champions with a 9-0-1 record. Athletics: Jim Ryun set a world record for running the mile in 3:51.3.

THEATRE: The original Broadway production of the musical *Cabaret* ran for 1,165 performances. One of the biggest flops in Broadway musical history, *Breakfast at Tiffany's* played 4 previews but never officially opened.

1967

BIRTHS: Kurt Cobain (February 20) was the singer, songwriter, and guitarist for Seattle, Washington's grunge rock band Nirvana, whose 2nd album, *Nevermind*, has sold over 30 million copies. Dara Torres (April 15) has won 12 Olympic swimming medals and is the only swimmer in U.S. history to compete in 5 Olympic Games (1984, 1988, 1992, 2000, and 2008). Actress Julia Roberts (October 28) won the Best Actress Academy Award for her performance in 2000's *Erin Brockovich* and has been named one of *People* magazine's '50 Most Beautiful People in the World' 11 times, tied with actress Halle Berry for most ever. Criss Angel (December 19) is a magician and illusionist who created the TV show *Criss Angel Mindfreak* and his live performance show at Las Vegas, Nevada's Luxor Casino.

ART & ARCHITECTURE: Pop artists Peter Blake and Jann Haworth created The Beatles' *Sgt. Pepper's Lonely Hearts Club Band* album cover. Other works produced include Andy Warhol's silk screen print *Big Electric Chair*, Barnett Newman's abstract painting *Voice of Fire* and Kenneth Snelson's stainless steel sculpture *Six Number Two*. Marina City, designed by Bertrand Goldberg, opened in Chicago, Illinois consisting of 2 corncob-shaped residential towers at 587 feet tall with 65 stories each.

FILM & TV: *In the Heat of the Night* won the Best Picture Academy Award and the Best Actor Oscar for Rod Steiger. Other top films were *The Graduate* starring Anne Bancroft and Dustin Hoffman; *Guess Who's Coming to Dinner* starring Spencer Tracy, Katherine Hepburn, and Sidney Poitier; *Cool Hand Luke* starring Paul Newman and George Kennedy (Best Supporting Actor Oscar); *Bonnie and Clyde* starring Warren Beatty and Faye Dunaway; *The Dirty Dozen* starring Lee Marvin and Ernest Borgnine; and *The Good, the Bad and the Ugly* starring Clint Eastwood, Lee Van Cleef, and Eli Wallach. Martin Sheen, Jon Voight, Harvey Keitel, Richard Dreyfuss, and Gene Wilder made their film debuts. TV show premieres included *The Flying Nun, Ironside, The Smothers Brothers Comedy Hour, Mannix,* and *The Carol Burnett Show.*

INDUSTRY: To compete with Ford's popular Mustang, General Motors introduced 2 new sports cars: the Chevrolet Camaro and the Pontiac Firebird. Fashion designer Ralph Lauren founded his own company famous for its Polo brand of clothing, accessories, and fragrances.

LITERATURE: S.E. Hinton was a 16-year-old junior in high school when she wrote *The Outsiders.* Other published works include *Rosemary's Baby* by Ira Levin, Scott O'Dell's *The Black Pearl*, Chaim Potok's *The Chosen,* and William Styron's Pulitzer Prize winning novel, *The Confessions of Nat Turner.*

MUSIC: The Beatles' "Michelle" won the Song of the Year Grammy Award. Other top songs were The Monkees' "I'm a Believer;" The Doors' "Light My Fire;" Sam and Dave's "Soul Man;" The Turtles' "Happy Together;" and Aretha Franklin's "Respect."

SPORTS: Baseball: The NL's St. Louis Cardinals defeated the AL's Boston Red Sox 4 games to 3 in the World Series. Red Sox left fielder Carl Yastrzemski won batting's Triple Crown. Football: The Green Bay Packers beat the Kansas City Chiefs 35-10 in Super Bowl I at the Los Angeles Memorial Coliseum, January 15. The University of Southern California Trojans were college football national champions with a 10-1 record.

1968

BIRTHS: James Todd Smith (January 14), better known as LL Cool J (**L**adies **L**ove **Cool J**ames), is a rapper who has released 13 albums since 1985 and is an actor on the crime drama TV series *NCIS: Los Angeles.* Professional skateboarder Tony Hawk (May 12) was the first person to complete a '900,' which is two-and-a-half mid-air revolutions on a skateboard. He has won 9 X Game gold medals. Rachael Ray (August 25) is a celebrity chef who hosts the Food Network TV series' *30 Minute Meals, Rachael Ray's Tasty Travels,* and *$40 a Day.* Will Smith (September 25) has gained success in TV, film, and music. He has starred in 4 films that have grossed over $500 million: *Independence Day, Men In Black, I Am Legend,* and *Hancock.*

ART & ARCHITECTURE: Donald De Lue's *Special Warfare Memorial Statue* was the first Vietnam Memorial in the U.S. Known informally as 'Bronze Bruce,' it is the centerpiece of Memorial Plaza at Fort Bragg, North Carolina. Designed by O'Neil Ford, the 750-foot tall Tower of the Americas was built for the 1968 World's Fair in San Antonio, Texas.

FILM & TV: *Oliver!* won the Best Picture Academy Award and the Best Director Oscar for Carol Reed. Other top films were *2001: A Space Odyssey; Funny Girl* starring Barbra Streisand and Omar Sharif; *Planet of the Apes* starring Charlton Heston, Roddy McDowall, and Kim Hunter; *The Odd Couple* starring Jack Lemmon and Walter Matthau; *Bullitt* starring Steve McQueen; *The Green Berets* starring John Wayne and David Janssen; *The Lion in Winter* starring Peter O'Toole and Katherine Hepburn; and *Rosemary's Baby* starring Mia Farrow, John Cassavetes, and Ruth Gordon. Robert De Niro, Goldie Hawn, Anthony Hopkins, and Martin Scorsese made their film debuts. TV show premieres included *Hawaii Five-O; The Mod Squad; 60 Minutes; Mister Rogers' Neighborhood; Laugh-In;* and *Adam-12.*

INDUSTRY: The Mattel Toy Company introduced Hot Wheels die cast toy cars. The first of the original 16 castings was a dark blue Chevrolet Camaro. K-tel perfected the TV infomercial by selling music compilation albums and household products. McDonald's created the Big Mac hamburger, which originally sold for 45 cents.

LITERATURE: Tom Wolfe's *The Electric Kool-Aid Acid Test* is the essential book about 1960s hippie culture. The 1982 film *Blade Runner* is based on Philip K. Dick's science fiction novel *Do Androids Dream of Electric Sheep?*

MUSIC: The 5th Dimension's "Up, Up and Away" won the Song of the Year Grammy Award. Bobbie Gentry won Best New Artist. Other top songs were Steppenwolf's "Born to Be Wild," Dusty Springfield's "Son of a Preacher Man," Canned Heat's "On the Road Again," Otis Redding's "(Sittin' On) The Dock of the Bay," and Louis Armstrong's "What a Wonderful World."

SPORTS: Baseball: The AL's Detroit Tigers defeated the NL's St. Louis Cardinals 4 games to 3 in the World Series. Football: The Green Bay Packers beat the Oakland Raiders 33-14 in Super Bowl II in Miami, Florida. The Ohio State University Buckeyes were college football national champions with a 10-0 record. USC Trojans running back O.J. Simpson won the Heisman Trophy. Golf: Bob Goalby won the Masters Tournament when Roberto DeVicenzo was disqualified for signing an incorrect scorecard.

THEATRE: The Broadway musical *Hair* broke new ground by using a racially integrated cast and inviting the audience onstage for the 'Be-In' finale.

1969

BIRTHS: Model Christy Turlington (January 2) has done print and TV ads for dozens of companies including Maybelline Cosmetics, and Versace. She represented Calvin Klein from 1987 to 2007. Brian Warner (January 5), better known as Marilyn Manson, is a musician famous for his elaborate theatrical performances. He has sold over 50 million albums worldwide. Actress Jennifer Aniston (February 11) is best known for portraying Rachel Green on the 1990s TV sitcom *Friends,* for which she earned $1.2 million per episode during its final season. Brett Favre (October 10) is a retired NFL quarterback who played most of his 20-year career for the Green Bay Packers. He holds the NFL career records for most touchdown passes (508), most passing yards (71,838), and most pass completions (6,300).

ART & ARCHITECTURE: Pop artist Andy Warhol founded *Interview* magazine, nicknamed 'The Crystal Ball of Pop.' Sculptor Alexander Calder created the 42-ton painted steel sculpture *La Grande Vitesse,* which stands outside the City Hall of Grand Rapids, Michigan. When Chicago's 100-story, 1,127-foot tall John Hancock Center was completed on May 6, it was the tallest building in the world outside New York City.

FILM & TV: *Midnight Cowboy* won the Best Picture Academy Award and the Best Director Oscar for John Schlesinger. Other top films were *Butch Cassidy and the Sundance Kid* starring Paul Newman and Robert Redford; *Easy Rider* starring Peter Fonda and Dennis Hopper; *The Wild Bunch* starring William Holden and Ernest Borgnine; *Paint Your Wagon* starring Lee Marvin and Clint Eastwood; *Cactus Flower* starring Walter Matthau, Ingrid Bergman, and Goldie Hawn; and *True Grit* starring John Wayne (Best Actor Oscar). Mel Brooks, Angelica Huston, Al Pacino, and Jeff Bridges made their film debuts. TV show premieres included *The Brady Bunch; Love: American Style; Marcus Welby, M.D.; Hee Haw;* and the TV show that more people in the world have watched than any other, *Sesame Street.*

INDUSTRY: Wendy's hamburger restaurant chain was founded in Columbus, Ohio. Parker Brothers sold more than 4 million Nerf Balls (a polyurethane foam ball safe for indoor use) in its first year of production.

LITERATURE: Maya Angelou's autobiography *I Know Why the Caged Bird Sings* details her rise above 1960s racial oppression. Mario Puzo's *The Godfather* introduced the Corleone New York Mafia crime family.

MUSIC: O.C. Smith's "Little Green Apples" won the Song of the Year Grammy Award. Jose Feliciano won Best New Artist. Other top songs were The Zombies' "Time of the Season;" Marvin Gaye's "I Heard it Through the Grapevine;" The 5th Dimension's "Aquarius;" Tommy James and the Shondells' "Crimson and Clover;" and The Archies' "Sugar, Sugar."

SPORTS: The NL's New York Mets defeated the AL's Baltimore Orioles 4 games to 1 in the World Series. Football: The New York Jets upset the heavily favored Baltimore Colts 16-7 in Super Bowl III. The University of Texas Longhorns were college football national champions with a 10-0 record. Hockey: Goalie Karen Koch became the world's first female professional hockey player when she signed a contract for $40 per game with the Marquette Iron Rangers.

THEATRE: Al Pacino won the Tony Award for Best Dramatic Actor in a Supporting Role for the Broadway play, *Does a Tiger Wear a Necktie?*

1970

On April 1, the U.S. population was 203,392,031 people. The average yearly income for a U.S. worker was $6,186, equal to $34,848 today; the average house cost $23,400, equal to $131,823 today; the average car cost $3,350, equal to $18,872 today; a gallon of gas cost 36 cents, equal to $2.02 today; and sirloin steak cost $1.19 per pound, equal to $6.70 today.

BIRTHS: Author Daniel Handler (February 28) is best known for his work written under the pen name, Lemony Snicket, such as *A Series of Unfortunate Events, Watch Your Mouth,* and *The Basic Eight.* Retired professional tennis player Andre Agassi (April 29) was the first of only 2 men to win the Career Golden Slam: all 4 grand slam tournaments plus an Olympic gold medal. Beck (July 8) is a singer-songwriter, producer, and multi-instrumentalist, known for combining many different musical styles. Giada De Larentiis (August 22) is a chef, writer, and host of the Food Network's TV cooking program *Giada at Home.*

ART: Cartoonist Gary Trudeau's comic strip *Doonesbury* debuted as a daily strip in about 2 dozen newspapers on October 26. Sculptor Robert Smithson constructed the *Spiral Jetty*, a 1,500-foot long counterclockwise coil made of rocks and earth jutting from the shore into the Great Salt Lake in Utah.

FILM & TV: *Patton* won the Best Picture Academy Award as well as the Best Director Oscar for Franklin J. Schaffner and the Best Actor Oscar for George C. Scott. Other top films were *Airport* starring Burt Lancaster and Dean Martin; *Love Story* starring Ryan O'Neal and Ali MacGraw; *MASH* starring Donald Sutherland and Elliott Gould; *Little Big Man* starring Dustin Hoffman and Faye Dunaway; and *Catch-22* starring Alan Arkin. Tommy Lee Jones, Diane Keaton, Sylvester Stallone, and Susan Sarandon made their film debuts. TV show premieres included *The Mary Tyler Moore Show; NFL Monday Night Football; The Odd Couple; McCloud; The Partridge Family; All My Children;* and *The Flip Wilson Show.*

INDUSTRY: The world's first jumbo jet, the Boeing 747, debuted on Pan Am's New York to London flight. The Public Broadcasting System (PBS) TV network was launched on October 5. Surfwear maker Quicksilver was founded in Huntington Beach, California.

LITERATURE: Richard Bach's *Jonathan Livingston Seagull* sat at the top of the *New York Times* Best Seller List for 38 consecutive weeks, selling over 1 million copies. Other published works include James Dickey's *Deliverance,* Albert Speer's *Inside the Third Reich,* and Alvin Toffler's *Future Shock.*

MUSIC: Joe South's "Games People Play" won the Song of the Year Grammy Award. Crosby, Stills & Nash won Best New Artist. Other top songs were Santana's "Black Magic Woman," The Jackson 5's "ABC," and Chicago's "I'm A Man." Jimi Hendrix died in London from an overdose of sleeping pills and Janis Joplin died in Los Angeles from a heroin overdose; both were just 27 years old.

SPORTS: Baseball: The AL's Baltimore Orioles defeated the NL's Cincinnati Reds 4 games to 1 in the World Series. Football: The Kansas City Chiefs beat the Minnesota Vikings 23-7 in Super Bowl IV. The University of Nebraska Cornhuskers were college football national champions with an 11-0-1 record. Hockey: The Boston Bruins swept the St. Louis Blues 4 games to 0 to win the Stanley Cup.

1971

BIRTHS: Sheryl Swoopes (March 25) was the first player signed by the Women's National Basketball Association, by the Houston Comets in 1997. She is a 3-time WNBA Most Valuable Player Award winner and has won 3 Olympic gold medals. Marc Andreessen (July 9) invented one of the first Internet web browsers, Netscape Navigator, in 1994. He is one of only six members of the World Wide Web Hall of Fame. Figure skater Kristi Yamaguchi (July 12) won the 1992 Olympic gold medal in ladies' singles. Cyclist Lance Armstrong (September 18) won the Tour de France a record 7 consecutive times from 1999 to 2005. However, the U.S. Anti-Doping Agency gave Armstrong a lifetime ban and disqualified all of his racing results when they charged him with doping in August, 2012.

ART: Artist Fritz Koenig created the bronze statue *The Sphere,* which originally stood between the World Trade Center twin towers in Manhattan but now is displayed in New York City's Battery Park as a memorial to the victims of 9/11.

FILM & TV: *The French Connection* won the Best Picture Academy Award as well as the Best Director Oscar for William Friedkin and the Best Actor Oscar for Gene Hackman. Other top films were *Fiddler on the Roof; Summer of '42* starring Jennifer O'Neill; *The Last Picture Show* starring Ben Johnson, Jeff Bridges and Cybill Shepherd; *Dirty Harry* starring Clint Eastwood; *Diamonds Are Forever* starring Sean Connery and Jill St. John; and *A Clockwork Orange* starring Malcolm McDowell. Morgan Freeman, Kathy Bates, Danny DeVito, Steven Spielberg, and George Lucas made their film debuts. TV show premieres included *All in the Family; Columbo; Masterpiece Theatre; The Electric Company; McMillan and Wife;* and *The Sonny and Cher Show.*

INDUSTRY: The Hard Rock Café theme restaurant chain was founded in London. The Starbucks coffeehouse chain started in Seattle, Washington and now has nearly 20,000 locations in 60 countries.

LITERATURE: Xaviera Hollander's *The Happy Hooker: My Own Story* described her work as a high-end prostitute in New York City during the late 1960s. Other works published include William Peter Blatty's *The Exorcist;* Frederick Forsyth's *The Day of the Jackal;* John Updike's *Rabbit Redux;* Herman Wouk's *The Winds of War;* and James Michener's *The Drifters.*

MUSIC: Simon & Garfunkel's "Bridge Over Troubled Water" won the Song of the Year Grammy Award. The Carpenters won Best New Artist. Other top songs were Three Dog Night's "Joy to the World;" Carole King's "It's Too Late;" Rod Stewart's "Maggie May;" Janis Joplin's "Me And Bobby McGee;" John Lennon's "Imagine;" and The Carpenters' "Superstar."

SPORTS: Baseball: The NL's Pittsburgh Pirates defeated the AL's Baltimore Orioles 4 games to 1 in the World Series. Game 4 at Pittsburgh's Three Rivers Stadium was the first night game in World Series history. Football: The Baltimore Colts beat the Dallas Cowboys 16-13 in Super Bowl V. The University of Nebraska Cornhuskers were college football champions with a 13-0 record. Boxing: Joe Frazier defeated Muhammad Ali March 8 at New York City's Madison Square Garden to retain the World Heavyweight Title.

THEATRE: When it closed in 1980 after 3,388 performances, the musical *Grease* had the longest run in Broadway history.

1972

BIRTHS: Shaquille O'Neal (March 6) is a former professional basketball player who is one of only 3 players to win the NBA MVP, All-Star Game MVP, and NBA Finals MVP awards in the same season (along with Willis Reed and Michael Jordan). Mia Hamm (March 17) is a retired professional soccer player who scored 158 international goals during her career, more than any other player, male or female, in the history of soccer. Actress Gwyneth Paltrow (September 27) won the Best Actress Academy Award for her performance in the 1998 film *Shakespeare in Love.* She is married to Chris Martin, lead singer for the rock band Coldplay. Rapper Eminem (October 17) was born Marshall Mathers III and has sold more than 100 million albums worldwide since 1992.

ART & ARCHITECTURE: *Earth Rise,* the most famous photograph of all time, was taken by the Apollo 17 crew during the last manned flight to the moon. Designed by architect William Pereira, the 48-story, 850-foot tall Transamerica Pyramid is the tallest skyscraper in San Francisco. The Phillips Exeter Academy Library in Exeter, New Hampshire, is the largest secondary school library in the world with nine floors and 160,000 volumes.

FILM & TV: *The Godfather* won the Best Picture Academy Award and the Best Actor Oscar for Marlon Brando. Other top films were *What's Up Doc?* starring Barbra Streisand and Ryan O'Neal; *The Poseidon Adventure* starring Gene Hackman and Ernest Borgnine; *Cabaret* starring Liza Minnelli (Best Actress Oscar) and Joel Grey (Best Supporting Actor Oscar); *Deliverance* starring Burt Reynolds and Jon Voight; and *Jeremiah Johnson* starring Robert Redford. Jodie Foster, Samuel L. Jackson, Sissy Spacek, and James Woods made their film debuts. TV show premieres included *Sanford and Son, The Bob Newhart Show, Maude, The Waltons,* and *M*A*S*H.*

INDUSTRY: Atari introduced *Pong,* the first commercially successful video game, which led to the start of the video game industry. The cable TV network HBO (Home Box Office) was launched by showing the film *Sometimes a Great Notion* followed by an NHL hockey game between the New York Rangers and Vancouver Canucks.

LITERATURE: Richard Adams' anthropomorphic fantasy novel *Watership Down* was rejected 13 times before finding a publisher. Other works published include Hunter S. Thompson's *Fear and Loathing in Las Vegas,* Ira Levin's *The Stepford Wives,* and Frederick Forsyth's *The Odessa File.*

MUSIC: Carole King's "You've Got a Friend" won the Song of the Year Grammy Award. Carly Simon won Best New Artist. Other top songs were Harry Nilsson's "Without You," Don McLean's "American Pie," Dr. Hook's "The Cover of the Rolling Stone," and Neil Young's "Heart of Gold."

SPORTS: Baseball: The AL's Oakland Athletics defeated the NL's Cincinnati Reds 4 games to 3 in the World Series. Football: The Dallas Cowboys beat the Miami Dolphins 24-3 in Super Bowl VI. The University of Southern California Trojans were college football national champions with a 12-0 record. Basketball: The Los Angeles Lakers defeated the New York Knicks 4 games to 1 to win the NBA Championship. Hockey: The Boston Bruins beat the New York Rangers 4 games to 2 to win the Stanley Cup.

THEATRE: Bob Fosse directed and choreographed the Broadway musical *Pippen,* which ran for 1,944 performances and starred John Rubinstein, Jill Clayburgh, and Ben Vereen.

1973

BIRTHS: Boxer Oscar De La Hoya (February 4) defeated 17 world champions and won 10 world titles in 6 different weight classes. He has generated more money than any other boxer in the history of the sport: $696 million from pay-per-view profits. Musician Rufus Wainwright (July 22) began playing the piano at age 6 and started touring with his family (father Loudon Wainwright III and sister Martha) at age 13. Seth MacFarlane (October 26) is a voice actor, animator, and producer best known for creating the animated TV series *Family Guy*. Model Tyra Banks (December 4) was the first African-American woman to appear on the cover of *GQ* magazine and the *Sports Illustrated Swimsuit Issue*. She is the creator and host of the reality TV show *America's Next Top Model*.

ART & ARCHITECTURE: Braniff International Airways commissioned artist Alexander Calder to paint a full size DC-8 airplane as a 'flying canvas.' Designed by architect Minoru Yamasaki, the 110-story, 1,368–foot tall World Trade Center Twin Towers opened April 4 in Manhattan's financial district. The Sears Tower in Chicago, Illinois became the tallest building in the world at 108 stories and 1,451 feet tall.

FILM & TV: *The Sting* won the Best Picture Academy Award as well as the Best Director Oscar for George Roy Hill. Other top films were *The Exorcist* starring Ellen Burstyn and Linda Blair; *Papillon* starring Steve McQueen and Dustin Hoffman; *The Way We Were* starring Robert Redford and Barbra Streisand; *American Graffiti* starring Richard Dreyfuss and Ron Howard; and *Magnum Force* starring Clint Eastwood. *Enter the Dragon* starring Bruce Lee was the first American made martial arts film. Nick Nolte, Bernadette Peters, and John Candy made their film debuts. TV show premieres included *Kojak, The Six Million Dollar Man, Barnaby Jones,* and *Schoolhouse Rock!*

INDUSTRY: Inspired by watching Captain Kirk use his communicator on the TV show *Star Trek,* Dr. Martin Cooper of Motorola invented the world's first cellular phone. He made the first cell phone call to his rival, Joel Engel, head of research at Bell Labs. NASA launched the Skylab space station on May 14.

LITERATURE: William Goldman's fantasy novel *The Princess Bride* was made into a 1987 film directed by Rob Reiner.

MUSIC: Roberta Flack's "The First Time Ever I Saw Your Face" won the Song of the Year Grammy Award. America won Best New Artist. Other top songs were Carly Simon's "You're So Vain;" The Carpenters' "Top of the World;" Stevie Wonder's "Superstition;" Todd Rundgren's "Hello, It's Me;" Aerosmith's "Dream On;" The Doobie Brothers' "China Grove;" Tony Orlando and Dawn's "Tie a Yellow Ribbon Round the Ole Oak Tree;" and Charlie Rich's "Behind Closed Doors."

SPORTS: Baseball: The AL's Oakland Athletics defeated the NL's New York Mets 4 games to 3 in the World Series. George Steinbrenner bought the New York Yankees for $10 million from CBS. Football: The Miami Dolphins completed the only unbeaten and untied season (17-0) in NFL history when they beat the Washington Redskins 14-7 in Super Bowl VII. Boxing: George Foreman knocked out Joe Frazier in the second round to become World Heavyweight Champion. Horse Racing: Secretariat won the U.S. Triple Crown, setting race records in all 3 events: the Kentucky Derby (1:59.4), the Preakness Stakes (1:53), and the Belmont Stakes (2:24); records that still stand today.

1974

BIRTHS: Jewel Kilcher (May 23) is a singer-songwriter whose 1995 debut album, *Pieces of You,* has sold over 15 million copies. Professional baseball player Derek Jeter (June 26) is the New York Yankees' all-time career leader in hits (3,294), games played (2,568), at bats (10,477), and stolen bases (348). He has won 5 World Series in 18 seasons with the Yankees, has been selected to 13 All-Star Games, and is MLB's career leader in hits by a shortstop. Actress Hillary Swank (July 30) has won the Best Actress Academy Award twice: for 1999's *Boys Don't Cry* and 2004's *Million Dollar Baby.* Actor Leonardo DiCaprio (November 11) has been nominated for 8 Golden Globe Awards, winning Best Actor for 2004's *The Aviator.*

FILM & TV: *The Godfather, Part II* won the Best Picture Academy Award and the best Director Oscar for Francis Ford Coppola. Other top films were *Blazing Saddles* starring Gene Wilder and Harvey Korman; *Earthquake* starring Charlton Heston and George Kennedy; *The Towering Inferno* starring Steve McQueen and Paul Newman; *Young Frankenstein* starring Gene Wilder and Peter Boyle; and *Chinatown* starring Jack Nicholson and Faye Dunaway. Richard Gere, Jeff Goldblum, and Denzel Washington made their film debuts. TV show premieres included *Happy Days* (which spawned a record 8 spin-off series); *Good Times; Little House on the Prairie; Rhoda; Chico and the Man; The Rockford Files; Land of the Lost;* and PBS' *Nova.*

INDUSTRY: Bob Taylor founded Taylor Guitars in El Cajon, California. Notable artists who play Taylor guitars include John Petrucci, Jason Mraz, and Taylor Swift. The Magna Doodle has sold over 40 million units worldwide, making it the number one drawing toy of all time.

LITERATURE: Peter Benchley's novel *Jaws* stayed on the *New York Times* Best Seller List for 44 weeks and eventually sold 20 million copies. Other works published include *All the President's Men* by Carl Bernstein and Bob Woodward; Erica Jong's *Fear of Flying; Helter Skelter* by Vincent Bugliosi; James Michener's *Centennial;* and *The Onion Field* by Joseph Wambaugh.

MUSIC: Roberta Flack's "Killing Me Softly With His Song" won the Song of the Year Grammy Award. Bette Midler won Best New Artist. Other top songs were Harry Chapin's "Cats in the Cradle;" Pink Floyd's "Money;" Marvin Hamlisch's "The Entertainer;" Carl Douglas' "Kung Fu Fighting;" Lynyrd Skynyrd's "Sweet Home Alabama;" Gordon Lightfoot's "Sundown;" Queen's "Killer Queen;" and Golden Earring's "Radar Love."

SPORTS: Baseball: The AL's Oakland Athletics defeated the NL's Los Angeles Dodgers 4 games to 1 in the World Series. Football: The Miami Dolphins beat the Minnesota Vikings 24-7 in Super Bowl VIII. The University of Oklahoma Sooners were college football national champions with an 11-0 record. Basketball: The Boston Celtics defeated the Milwaukee Bucks 4 games to 3 to win the NBA Championship. The UCLA Bruins record streak of 7 consecutive national titles ended when the North Carolina State University Wolfpack beat the Marquette University Golden Eagles 76-64 in the NCAA men's basketball tournament. Hockey: The Philadelphia Flyers won the Stanley Cup by defeating the Boston Bruins 4 games to 2. The University of Minnesota Golden Gophers beat the Michigan Technological University Huskies 4-2 to win the NCAA men's hockey championship.

1975

BIRTHS: Drew Barrymore (February 22) is a member of the famous Barrymore acting family (her grandfather was John Barrymore). Her breakout role came in 1982's *E.T. the Extra Terrestrial.* Lauryn Hill (May 25) is a singer-songwriter whose first album, *The Miseducation of Lauryn Hill* won 5 Grammy Awards including Album of the Year and has sold 19 million copies. Musician Jack White (July 9) is a multi-instrumentalist best known for creating the band The White Stripes. He produced country singer Loretta Lynn's 2004 Grammy Award winning album *Van Lear Rose.* Tiger Woods (December 30) has won 101 professional golf tournaments since 1996, earning more than $100 million in prize money and has been awarded the PGA Player of the Year a record 10 times.

ART: T.E. Breitenbach painted the oil painting *Proverbidioms,* which depicts over 300 common proverbs, catchphrases, and clichés such as 'you are what you eat,' 'a frog in the throat,' and 'kicked the bucket.' Roy Lichtenstein created the pop art painting *Cubist Still Life with Lemons.*

FILM & TV: *One Flew Over the Cuckoo's Nest* became only the second film in Hollywood history (1934's *It Happened One Night* was the first) to win all 5 major Academy Awards: Best Picture, Best Director (Milos Forman), Best Actor (Jack Nicholson), Best Actress (Louise Fletcher), and Best Screenplay. Other top films were *Jaws* starring Roy Scheider and Robert Shaw; *Shampoo* starring Warren Beatty and Julie Christie; *Dog Day Afternoon* starring Al Pacino and John Cazale; *The Rocky Horror Picture Show* starring Tim Curry and Susan Sarandon; and *Three Days of the Condor* starring Robert Redford and Faye Dunaway. John Travolta, Bill Murray, Dennis Quaid, Joe Pesci, and Laurence Fishburne made their film debuts. TV show premieres included *Welcome Back, Kotter; The Jeffersons; Barney Miller; One Day at a Time; Baretta; Wheel of Fortune;* and *Good Morning America.*

INDUSTRY: Bill Gates and Paul Allen founded Microsoft, the world's largest software manufacturer, in Albuquerque, New Mexico. George Lucas created the motion picture visual effects company Industrial Light & Magic when he began production of the film *Star Wars.* Gary Dahl invented the pet rock, a fad that lasted only 6 months, but still made him a millionaire.

LITERATURE: Works published include James Clavell's 1200 page novel *Shogun;* E.L. Doctorow's *Ragtime;* Stephen King's *Salem's Lot;* Thomas Harris' *Black Sunday;* and Jack Higgins' *The Eagle Has Landed.*

MUSIC: Barbra Streisand's "The Way We Were" won the Song of the Year Grammy Award. Marvin Hamlisch won Best New Artist. Other top songs were Captain & Tennille's "Love Will Keep Us Together," Barry Manilow's "Mandy," Van McCoy's "The Hustle," and Glen Campbell's "Rhinestone Cowboy."

SPORTS: Baseball: The NL's Cincinnati Reds defeated the AL's Boston Red Sox 4 games to 3 in the World Series. Football: The Pittsburgh Steelers beat the Minnesota Vikings 16-6 in Super Bowl IX. The University of Oklahoma Sooners were college football national champions with an 11-1 record. Boxing: Regarded as the greatest fight in boxing history, *The Thrilla in Manila* had Muhammad Ali beating Joe Frazier in 14 rounds to retain the World Heavyweight Championship Title.

THEATRE: Bob Fosse choreographed the Broadway musical *Chicago,* which ran for 936 performances and starred Chita Rivera and Jerry Orbach.

1976

BIRTHS: Reese Witherspoon (March 22) won every major Best Actress award (Academy Award, Golden Globe, BAFTA, and Screen Actors Guild) for her portrayal of June Carter Cash in the 2005 film *Walk the Line.* Tim Duncan (April 25) is a professional basketball player for the San Antonio Spurs. He has won 4 NBA Championships, 3 NBA Finals MVP Awards, and is a 13-time NBA All-Star. Pat Tillman (November 6) left his career as a professional football player to enlist in the U.S. Army after the terrorist attacks of September 11, 2001. He died as a result of friendly fire in Afghanistan in 2004. Jack Dorsey (November 19) is a web developer who created the social networking service Twitter. He has a net worth of over $1.12 billion.

ARCHITECTURE: Designed by I.M. Pei, the 60-story, 790-foot tall John Hancock Tower is the tallest building in Boston and all of New England.

FILM & TV: *Rocky* won the Best Picture Academy Award and the Best Director Oscar for John Avildsen. Other top films were *A Star is Born* starring Barbra Streisand and Kris Kristofferson; *Silver Streak* starring Gene Wilder and Richard Pryor; *King Kong* starring Jeff Bridges and Jessica Lange; *The Bad News Bears* starring Walter Matthau and Tatum O'Neal; *Taxi Driver* starring Robert De Niro and Jodie Foster; *The Omen* starring Gregory Peck and Lee Remick; and *The Outlaw Josey Wales* starring Clint Eastwood. Albert Brooks, Tim Robbins, Brook Shields, James Cromwell, and Treat Williams made their film debuts. TV show premieres included *Laverne and Shirley; The Muppet Show; Charlie's Angels; Family Feud;* and *The Bionic Woman.*

INDUSTRY: Steve Jobs and Steve Wozniak were paid $750 for designing the prototype for the Atari video game, Breakout. The Liz Claiborne fashion company had sales of $2 million in its first year.

LITERATURE: Works published include Alex Haley's *Roots,* Anne Rice's *Interview with the Vampire,* and Ira Levin's *The Boys from Brazil.*

MUSIC: Judy Collins' "Send in the Clowns" won the Song of the Year Grammy Award. Natalie Cole won Best New Artist. Other top songs were Rod Stewart's "Tonight's The Night;" Wild Cherry's "Play That Funky Music;" Chicago's "If You Leave Me Now;" John Sebastian's "Welcome Back;" Paul McCartney & Wings' "Silly Love Songs;" The Bellamy Brothers' "Let Your Love Flow;" and Starland Vocal Band's "Afternoon Delight."

SPORTS: Baseball: The NL's Cincinnati Red swept the AL's New York Yankees 4 games to 0 in the World Series. Football: The Pittsburgh Steelers beat the Dallas Cowboys 21-17 in Super Bowl X. The University of Pittsburgh Panthers were college football national champions with a 12-0 record. Basketball: The Boston Celtics defeated the Phoenix Suns 4 games to 2 in the NBA Finals. The Indiana University Hoosiers beat the University of Michigan Wolverines 86-68 to win the NCAA men's basketball tournament. Motor Racing: Johnny Rutherford won the Indianapolis 500 in a rain-shortened 255-mile race. Olympics: Bruce Jenner won the gold medal for decathlon at the summer games in Montreal, Canada. Dorothy Hamill won the gold medal for Ladies' Singles Figure Skating in Innsbruck, Austria.

1977

BIRTHS: Chad Hurley (January 24) is the co-founder and former Chief Executive Officer of the video sharing website YouTube. In 2006, he and Steve Chen sold YouTube to Google for $1.65 billion. Misty May-Treanor (July 30) won 3 consecutive Olympic gold medals (2004, 2008, 2012) in beach volleyball with her teammate Kerri Walsh Jennings. She is the most successful female beach volleyball player of all time with 112 individual championship wins worldwide. Tom Brady (August 3) plays quarterback for the NFL's New England Patriots, leading them to 5 Super Bowls in 10 years, winning 3. He is married to supermodel Giselle Bundchen. Fiona Apple (September 13) is a singer-songwriter whose 1996 debut album *Tidal* has sold more than 3 million copies in the U.S.

ART & ARCHITECTURE: Sculptor Walter De Maria created the land art piece *The Lightning Field* in New Mexico, consisting of 400 stainless steel poles arranged in a 1 mile x 1 kilometer rectangular grid. The 59-story, 915-foot tall Citigroup Center is New York City's 8th tallest skyscraper, featuring a unique stilt-style base and a 45 degree slanted roof. Detroit's Renaissance Center is the world headquarters of General Motors and the tallest building in Michigan at 727 feet tall with 73 floors.

FILM & TV: *Annie Hall* won the Best Picture Academy Award as well as the Best Director Oscar for Woody Allen and the Best Actress Oscar for Diane Keaton. Other top films were *Star Wars* starring Mark Hamill and Harrison Ford; *Close Encounters of the Third Kind* starring Richard Dreyfuss and Terri Garr; *Smokey and the Bandit* starring Burt Reynolds, Sally Field, and Jackie Gleason; and *Saturday Night Fever* starring John Travolta. Meryl Streep, Mel Gibson, Sigourney Weaver, and Brian Dennehy made their film debuts. TV show premieres included *Soap; Three's Company; The Love Boat; Eight is Enough; Lou Grant;* and *CHiPs.*

INDUSTRY: The world's first space shuttle, *Enterprise,* made its first test flights in California. Originally named Constitution, a write-in campaign by *Star Trek* fans convinced NASA to change the name. The NASA space probes *Voyager I* and *II* were launched containing a gold disc etched with information about Earth, including Chuck Berry's song "Johnny B. Goode." The Apple II microcomputer with color graphics went on sale for $1,298.

LITERATURE: Stephen King took the title for his 3rd novel *The Shining* from a line in John Lennon's song "Instant Karma." Other works published include Colleen McCullough's *The Thorn Birds,* and Toni Morrison's *Song of Solomon.*

MUSIC: Barry Manilow's "I Write the Songs" won the Song of the Year Grammy Award. Starland Vocal Band won Best New Artist. Other top songs were Hall & Oates "Rich Girl;" Jimmy Buffett's "Margaritaville;" Stevie Wonder's "Sir Duke;" Manfred Mann's "Blinded by the Light;" The Eagles' "Hotel California;" and Debby Boone's "You Light Up My Life." 42-year-old Elvis Presley was found dead on the bathroom floor of his Graceland mansion from an overdose of prescription pills on August 16.

SPORTS: Baseball: The AL's New York Yankees defeated the NL's Los Angeles Dodgers 4 games to 2 in the World Series when Yankee slugger Reggie Jackson earned the nickname 'Mr. October.' Football: The Oakland Raiders beat the Minnesota Vikings 32-14 in Super Bowl XI.

THEATRE: The original production of the Broadway musical *Annie* ran for nearly 6 years and 2,377 performances.

1978

BIRTHS: Karina Smirnoff (January 2) is a professional ballroom dancer who has won the U.S. National Dance Championship 5 times and has starred in the TV show *Dancing with the Stars* since 2006, winning season 13 with Army veteran J.R. Martinez. Professional basketball player Kobe Bryant (August 23) has won 5 NBA Finals titles playing guard for the Los Angeles Lakers and is a 14-time NBA All-Star. Bubba Watson (November 5) is a pro golfer who won the Masters Tournament in 2012. He can hit a golf ball over 350 yards, generating a ball speed of 194 miles per hour. Singer-songwriter John Legend (December 28) has won 9 Grammy Awards in R&B, Soul, Rap, and Jazz Fusion musical genres.

ART: Jim Davis created *Garfield,* which holds the Guinness World Record for being the most widely syndicated comic strip ever, appearing in 2,580 newspapers worldwide.

FILM & TV: *The Deer Hunter* won the Best Picture Academy Award as well as the Best Director Oscar for Michael Cimino and the Best Supporting Actor Oscar for Christopher Walken. Other top films were *Grease* starring John Travolta and Olivia Newton-John; *Superman* starring Christopher Reeve and Gene Hackman; *Halloween* starring Jamie Lee Curtis and Donald Pleasence; *Foul Play* starring Goldie Hawn and Chevy Chase; *Up in Smoke* starring Cheech Marin and Tommy Chong; and *Animal House* starring John Belushi. Kevin Bacon, Karen Allen, Billy Crystal, Daryl Hannah, Ed Harris, Mark Harmon, Liam Neeson, and Mary Steenburgen made their film debuts. TV show premieres included *Dallas; Mork & Mindy; Taxi; WKRP in Cincinnati; The Incredible Hulk; Fantasy Island; 20/20;* and *Battlestar Galactica.*

INDUSTRY: Kenner introduced their line of *Star Wars* toys, the most successful movie licensed properties of all time. Milton Bradley launched the memory skill game *Simon* at Studio 54 in New York City. Ben Cohen and Jerry Greenfield founded Ben & Jerry's Ice Cream Company after completing a correspondence course on ice cream making from Pennsylvania State University's Creamery. The Volkswagen Rabbit became the first foreign car to be manufactured in the U.S.

LITERATURE: Christina Crawford, the adopted daughter of actress Joan Crawford, wrote one of the first celebrity tell-all books, *Mommie Dearest.* Other published works include John Irving's *The World According to Garp;* Herman Wouk's *War and Remembrance;* Christopher Koch's *The Year of Living Dangerously;* and Stephen King's *The Stand.*

MUSIC: Barbra Streisand's "Evergreen (Love Theme from *A Star Is Born*)" won the Song of the Year Grammy Award. Debby Boone won Best New Artist. Other top songs were The Bee Gees' "Night Fever" and "Stayin' Alive;" The Village People's "Y.M.C.A.;" Player's "Baby Come Back;" Andy Gibb's "Shadow Dancing;" Chic's "Le Freak;" and Exile's "Kiss You All Over."

SPORTS: Baseball: The World Series had the same result as the previous year: Yankees over Dodgers 4 games to 2. Football: The Dallas Cowboys beat the Denver Broncos 27-10 in Super Bowl XII. Horse Racing: Affirmed became the 11th and most recent winner of the U.S. Triple Crown.

THEATRE: Sam Shepard's play *Buried Child* won the Pulitzer Prize for Drama. *Ain't Misbehavin'* won Tony Awards for Best Musical and Best Performance by a Featured Actress in a Musical for Nell Carter.

1979

BIRTHS: Norah Jones (March 30) is a singer-songwriter whose 2002 debut album *Come Away with Me* won 5 Grammy Awards and has sold more than 26 million copies. She is the daughter of Indian sitar player Ravi Shankar. Claire Danes (April 12) has won several acting awards for her portrayal of CIA officer Carrie Mathison on the series *Homeland,* on cable TV's Showtime network. Carl Edwards (August 15) is a NASCAR driver who has won 63 professional races since 2003. He currently drives the #99 Ford Fusion in the Sprint Cup Series for Roush Fenway Racing. Sean Parker (December 3) has a net worth of $2.1 billion from co-founding the file-sharing computer service Napster and serving as the first president of the social networking website Facebook.

ART: Pop artist Roy Lichtenstein created the sculpture *Mermaid,* which is composed of concrete, steel, polyurethane, enamel, palm tree, and water. It is located outside the Jackie Gleason Theater in Miami Beach, Florida. The Albert Einstein Memorial, a bronze statue created by sculptor Robert Berks, sits on the grounds of Washington D.C.'s National Academy of Sciences.

FILM & TV: *Kramer vs. Kramer* won the Best Picture Academy Award as well as the Best Director Oscar for Robert Benton, the Best Actor Oscar for Dustin Hoffman, and the Best Supporting Actress Oscar for Meryl Streep. Other top films were *Apocalypse Now* starring Marlon Brando and Martin Sheen; *Star Trek: The Motion Picture* starring William Shatner and Leonard Nimoy; and *Alien* starring Sigourney Weaver. Mickey Roarke, Diane Lane, Patrick Swayze, Rosanna Arquette, and Danny Glover made their film debuts. TV show premieres included *The Dukes of Hazzard; Knots Landing; Benson; Hart to Hart;* and *Nightline.* ESPN, the world's first all sports TV network, was launched September 7 with the news of Chris Evert's tennis victory over Billie Jean King at the U.S. Open.

INDUSTRY: Bob and Harvey Weinstein named Miramax Films from combining the first names of their parents, Miriam and Max. Pixar Animation Studios was founded in Emeryville, California. Boba Fett, a *Star Wars* action figure sold by Kenner, was the top toy of 1979.

LITERATURE: Tom Wolfe's *The Right Stuff* detailed NASA's astronaut training program of the Mercury Project.

MUSIC: Billy Joel's "Just the Way You Are" won the Song of the Year Grammy Award. A Taste of Honey won Best New Artist. Other top songs were Blondie's "Heart of Glass" and "One Way or Another;" Gloria Gaynor's "I Will Survive;" Donna Summer's "Hot Stuff" and "Bad Girls;" The Knack's "My Sharona;" Al Stewart's "Time Passages;" and The Cars' "Let's Go."

SPORTS: Baseball: The NL's Pittsburgh Pirates defeated the AL's Baltimore Orioles 4 games to 3 in the World Series. Football: The Pittsburgh Steelers beat the Dallas Cowboys 35-31 in Super Bowl XIII. Basketball: The Michigan State University Spartans (led by Earvin 'Magic' Johnson) defeated the Indiana State University Sycamores (led by Larry Bird) 75-64 in the NCAA men's basketball tournament final. Rick Swenson won his 2nd of a record 5 Iditarod Sled Dog Race Championships in Alaska – led by his lead dogs Andy and O.B. (Old Buddy).

THEATRE: *The Elephant Man* won the Tony Award for Best Play and *Sweeney Todd: The Demon Barber of Fleet Street* won Best Musical.

1980

On April 1, the U.S. population was 226,545,805 people. The average yearly income for a U.S. worker was $12,513, equal to $33,235 today; the average house cost $64,000, equal to $171,579 today; the average car cost $7,200, equal to $19,123 today; a gallon of gas cost $1.25, equal to $3.32 today; and ground beef cost $1.39 per pound, equal to $3.69 today.

BIRTHS: Actor Jason James Richter (January 29) starred in the 1993 film *Free Willy*, when he was selected from more than 4,000 candidates to play the lead role of Jesse. Professional tennis player Venus Williams (June 17) has won 43 Women's Tennis Association singles titles, which ranks number 6 all-time. She is also ranked number 2 on the all-time career prize money earned list with over $28 million, behind her younger sister Serena. Figure skater Michelle Kwan (July 7) won 2 Olympic Medals and 5 World Championships during her career. Actor Macaulay Culkin (August 26) starred in the *Home Alone* film series and during the early 1990s he was considered the most successful child star since Shirley Temple.

FILM & TV: *Ordinary People* won the Best Picture Academy Award as well as the Best Director Oscar for Robert Redford and the Best Supporting Actor Oscar for Timothy Hutton. Other top films were *The Empire Strikes Back* starring Mark Hamill and Harrison Ford; *Stir Crazy* starring Gene Wilder and Richard Pryor; *Airplane!* starring Robert Hays and Julie Hagerty; *Coal Miner's Daughter* starring Sissy Spacek and Tommy Lee Jones; and *The Blues Brothers* starring John Belushi and Dan Aykroyd. Tom Hanks, Bruce Willis, Michael J. Fox, Michelle Pfeiffer, and Robin Williams made their film debuts. TV show premieres included *Magnum, P.I.*; *Bosom Buddies*; and *Solid Gold*.

INDUSTRY: 350 million Rubik's Cubes have been sold worldwide, making it the all time best-selling toy. Namco launched Pac-Man, which has become the highest-grossing video game ever, taking in an estimated 10 billion quarters ($2.5 billion). Invented by Art Fry of the 3M Company, the 3-inch square, canary yellow piece of stationery called Post-it Notes debuted in U.S. stores. Sony introduced the first Walkman portable cassette player at a price of $200. Ten years later they had sold 50 million players.

LITERATURE: Carl Sagan's *Cosmos* spent 70 weeks on the *New York Times* Best Seller List and has become the best-selling science book of all time.

MUSIC: The Doobie Brothers' "What a Fool Believes" won the Song of the Year Grammy Award. Rickie Lee Jones won Best New Artist. Other top songs were Lipps Inc's "Funkytown," Michael Jackson's "Rock with You," Blondie's "Call Me," and Diana Ross' "Upside Down." John Lennon was shot to death by a crazed fan on December 8 outside his apartment in New York City.

SPORTS: The NL's Philadelphia Phillies defeated the AL's Kansas City Royals 4 games to 2 in the World Series. Football: The Pittsburgh Steelers beat the Los Angeles Rams 31-19 in Super Bowl XIV. Hockey: The U.S. men's 'Miracle on Ice' Olympic hockey team pulled off the greatest upset in American sports history when they beat the USSR 4-3 in the medal round. Announcer Al Michaels gave the best sports call ever as time ran down... "11 seconds, you've got 10 seconds, the countdown going on right now! Morrow, up to Silk. 5 seconds left in the game. *Do you believe in miracles?! YES!*" The Americans captured the gold medal 2 days later by defeating Finland 4-2.

THEATRE: The Broadway musical *42nd Street* ran for 3,486 performances and won the Tony Award for Best Musical.

1981

BIRTHS: Paris Hilton (February 17), the great-granddaughter of Hilton Hotel founder Conrad Hilton, is a reality TV star and fashion designer whose products such as handbags, watches, and shoes generate more than $10 million a year in sales. Singer Beyonce Knowles (September 4) has been nominated for 43 Grammy Awards, winning 16, and is 1 of only 3 artists to have their first 4 albums debut atop the Billboard charts. Serena Williams (September 26) is a professional tennis player who has won 4 Olympic gold medals and over $40 million in prize money, making her the highest earning female athlete of all time. Entertainer Britney Spears (December 2) has won 228 awards, sold over 100 million albums worldwide, and received a star on Hollywood's Walk of Fame at the age of 21.

FILM & TV: *Chariots of Fire* won the Best Picture Academy Award. Other top films were *Raiders of the Lost Ark* starring Harrison Ford and Karen Allen; *On Golden Pond* starring Henry Fonda (Best Actor Oscar) and Katherine Hepburn (Best Actress Oscar); *Arthur* starring Dudley Moore and Liza Minnelli; *Stripes* starring Bill Murray and Harold Ramis; and *The Cannonball Run* starring Burt Reynolds and Dom Deluise. Tom Cruise, Kevin Costner, Meg Ryan, Sean Penn, Demi Moore, and Jeff Daniels made their film debuts. TV show premieres included *Dynasty; Hill Street Blues; SCTV; The Fall Guy; Simon & Simon; Gimme a Break;* and *Falcon Crest.*

INDUSTRY: IBM began selling its first Personal Computer, the 5150 with 64K bytes of memory for $3,000. NASA's first Space Shuttle capable of space flight, *Columbia,* orbited the Earth 36 times over 2 days on its maiden flight April 12. Konami introduced the arcade game *Frogger,* which has sold more than 20 million copies worldwide.

LITERATURE: Works published include Paul Theroux's *The Mosquito Coast;* Martin Cruz Smith's *Gorky Park;* Thomas Harris' *Red Dragon;* John Irving's *Hotel New Hampshire;* and Stephen King's *Cujo.*

MUSIC: Christopher Cross won Best New Artist and Song of the Year for "Sailing." Other top songs were Soft Cell's "Tainted Love;" Rick Springfield's "Jesse's Girl;" Hall & Oates' "Private Eyes" and "Kiss On My List;" Kool & the Gang's "Celebration;" The J. Geils Band' "Centerfold;" The Talking Heads' "Once in a Lifetime;" REO Speedwagon's "Keep on Loving You;" Prince's "Controversy;" Devo's "Whip It;" John Lennon's "Woman;" and Bruce Springsteen's "The River." Van Halen guitarist Eddie Van Halen married actress Valerie Bertinelli on April 11. An estimated 500,000 people attended a free concert by Simon & Garfunkel in New York's Central Park on September 19.

SPORTS: Baseball: The NL's Los Angeles Dodgers defeated the AL's New York Yankees 4 games to 2 in the World Series. Football: The Oakland Raiders beat the Philadelphia Eagles 27-10 in Super Bowl XV. The Clemson University Tigers were college football national champions with a 12-0 record. Hockey: The New York Islanders beat the Minnesota North Stars 4 games to 1 to win the Stanley Cup. Boxing: Sugar Ray Leonard retained his World Welterweight Title by knocking out Thomas Hearns in the 14th round. Tennis: John McEnroe defeated Sweden's Bjorn Borg at Wimbledon and the U.S. Open. Skiing: Phil Mahre was the men's overall season champion in the Alpine Skiing World Cup.

1982

BIRTHS: Racecar driver Danica Patrick (March 25) is the only woman to win an IndyCar Series race (the 2008 Indy Japan 300) and is the highest woman finisher at the Indianapolis 500 (3rd place in 2009). Kelly Clarkson (April 24) is a 2-time Grammy Award winning singer-songwriter who also won the first season of TV's *American Idol*. Speed skater Apolo Anton Ohno (May 22) is the most decorated American Winter Olympic athlete of all time, winning 8 medals (2 gold, 2 silver, and 4 bronze). Swimmer Natalie Coughlin (August 23) is a 12-time Olympic medalist who became the first woman to ever swim the 100-meter backstroke in under a minute.

ARCHITECTURE: Architect Maya Lin beat out 1,441 other submissions to win a public design competition for the Vietnam Veterans Memorial in Washington D.C. when she was 21 years old. The black granite V-shaped wall is etched with the names of 58,195 fallen soldiers carved into its face. It was ranked #10 on the American Institute of Architects 2007 list of 'America's Favorite Memorials.'

FILM & TV: *Gandhi* won the Best Picture Academy Award as well as the Best Director Oscar for Richard Attenborough and the Best Actor Oscar for Ben Kingsley. Other top films were *Tootsie* starring Dustin Hoffman and Jessica Lange (Best Supporting Actress Oscar); *An Officer and a Gentleman* starring Richard Gere, Debra Winger, and Louis Gossett, Jr. (Best Supporting Actor Oscar); *48 Hours* starring Nick Nolte and Eddie Murphy in his film debut; *Rocky III* starring Sylvester Stallone and Mr. T; and Steven Spielberg's *E.T. the Extra Terrestrial.* Glenn Close, Kevin Kline, Angelina Jolie, Gary Oldman, and Forest Whitaker made their film debuts. TV show premieres included *Cheers; Family Ties; Newhart; Night Rider; T.J. Hooker; St. Elsewhere; Silver Spoons;* and *Late Night with David Letterman.*

INDUSTRY: EPCOT Center (an acronym for Experimental Prototype Community of Tomorrow) opened at Disney World in Orlando, Florida. Barney Clark survived for 112 days after receiving the world's first artificial heart implant, the Jarvik-7. The DeLorean Motor Company (famous for its model DMC-12 that was used as the time travel vehicle in the *Back to the Future* film trilogy) went bankrupt, losing 2,500 jobs and over $100 million in investment money.

LITERATURE: Alice Walker's novel *The Color Purple* won the Pulitzer Prize for Fiction and the National Book Award for Fiction.

MUSIC: Kim Carnes' "Bette Davis Eyes" won the Song of the Year Grammy Award. Sheena Easton won Best New Artist. Other top songs were Survivor's "Eye of the Tiger;" Joan Jett and the Blackhearts' "I Love Rock 'n' Roll;" John Cougar's "Jack and Diane;" Steve Miller Band's "Abracadabra;" and Toto's "Rosanna." Michael Jackson's album *Thriller* went on to become the biggest-selling album of all time, with 110 million copies sold worldwide.

SPORTS: Baseball: The NL's St. Louis Cardinals defeated the AL's Milwaukee Brewers 4 games to 3 in the World Series. Football: The San Francisco 49ers beat the Cincinnati Bengals 26-21 in Super Bowl XVI. Basketball: The Los Angeles Lakers defeated the Philadelphia 76ers 4 games to 2 in the NBA Finals. The University of North Carolina Tar Heels beat the Georgetown University Hoyas 63-62 to win the NCAA men's basketball tournament.

THEATRE: The musical *Cats* debuted on October 8 and became the longest-running musical in Broadway history when it closed 18 years later on September 10, 2000 after a total of 7,485 performances.

1983

BIRTHS: Singer-songwriter Carrie Underwood (March 10) won the 4th season of TV's *American Idol* and her 2005 album *Some Hearts* is the best-selling female debut album in country music history, selling more than 7 million U.S. copies. Jessica Lynch (April 26) was a U.S. Army soldier whose 2003 rescue in Iraq was the first successful rescue of an American prisoner of war since World War II. Actress Mila Kunis (August 14) is best known for playing Jackie Burkhart on the TV series *That 70s Show* and for providing the voice of Meg Griffin on the TV animated show *Family Guy.* Jonah Hill (December 20) was nominated for a Best Supporting Actor Academy Award for his performance in the 2011 film *Moneyball.*

FILM & TV: *Terms of Endearment* won the Best Picture Academy Award as well as the Best Director Oscar for James L. Brooks, the Best Actress Oscar for Shirley MacLaine, and the Best Supporting Actor Oscar for Jack Nicholson. Other top films were *Return of the Jedi* starring Mark Hamill and Harrison Ford; *Trading Places* starring Dan Aykroyd and Eddie Murphy; *Risky Business* starring Tom Cruise and Rebecca De Mornay; *Mr. Mom* starring Michael Keaton and Terri Garr; *WarGames* starring Matthew Broderick and Dabney Coleman; *The Big Chill* starring Glenn Close and William Hurt; *Sudden Impact* starring Clint Eastwood; and *Flashdance* starring Jennifer Beals. John Cusack, Ray Liotta, Nicole Kidman, Kiefer Sutherland, Juliette Binoche, and Rob Lowe made their film debuts. TV show premieres included *The A-Team, Mama's Family, Webster, AfterMASH,* and *Fraggle Rock.*

INDUSTRY: Sony introduced the CDP-101, the world's first Compact Disc Player at a price of $730, alongside the first album to be released on CD, Billy Joel's *52nd Street.* Hooters restaurant chain, featuring young, attractive waitresses dressed in revealing outfits, was founded in Clearwater, Florida.

MUSIC: Willie Nelson's "Always on my Mind" won the Song of the Year Grammy Award. Men at Work won Best New Artist. Other top songs were Michael Jackson's "Billie Jean" and "Beat It;" Prince's "Little Red Corvette" and "1999;" Madonna's "Borderline;" ZZ Top's "Gimme All Your Lovin;" John Mellencamp's "Pink Houses;" and R.E.M.'s "Radio Free Europe." Paul Simon married actress Carrie Fisher on August 16.

SPORTS: Baseball: The AL's Baltimore Orioles defeated the NL's Philadelphia Phillies 4 games to 1 in the World Series. Football: The Washington Redskins beat the Miami Dolphins 27-17 in Super Bowl XVII. The Michigan Panthers won the first United States Football League (USFL) Championship over the Philadelphia Stars 24-22. The University of Miami Hurricanes won the first of their 5 college football national championships by defeating the University of Nebraska Cornhuskers 31-30 in the Orange Bowl. Basketball: The Philadelphia 76ers swept the Los Angeles Lakers 4 games to 0 to win the NBA Finals. The University of North Carolina State Wolfpack beat the University of Houston Cougars 54-52 to win the men's NCAA basketball tournament. Hockey: The New York Islanders swept the Edmonton Oilers 4 games to 0 to win the Stanley Cup.

THEATRE: The Broadway musical *La Cage aux Folles* ran for 4 years and 1,761 performances. It won 6 Tony Awards including Best Musical, Best Lead Actor in a Musical for George Hearn, Best Original Score for Jerry Herman, and Best Book of a Musical for Harvey Fierstein.

1984

BIRTHS: Mark Zuckerberg (May 14) is the co-founder, chairman, and Chief Executive Officer of the social networking website Facebook. He became a billionaire by the age of 23 and currently has a net worth of $9.4 billion. Singer Katy Perry (October 25) is the only female to have an album produce 5 number one singles (2010's *Teenage Dream*). Actress Scarlett Johansson (November 22) received a Best Actress BAFTA Award for her portrayal of Charlotte in the 2003 film *Lost in Translation* and a 2010 Best Actress Tony Award for her performance in the Arthur Miller play *A View From the Bridge*. LeBron James (December 30) is a professional basketball player for the 2012 NBA champion Miami Heat. He has won the NBA Rookie of the Year Award, the NBA Finals MVP Award, and 3 NBA MVP Awards.

ART: Sculptor Frederick Hart created *The Three Soldiers*, a bronze statue depicting 3 young U.S. soldiers from the Vietnam War era. It was designed to compliment the Vietnam Veterans Memorial in Washington, D.C.

FILM & TV: *Amadeus* won the Best Picture Academy Award as well as the Best Director Oscar for Milos Forman and the Best Actor Oscar for F. Murray Abraham. Other top films were *Beverly Hills Cop* starring Eddie Murphy; *The Karate Kid* starring Ralph Macchio, Pat Morita, and Elizabeth Shue; *Ghostbusters* starring Bill Murray, Dan Aykroyd, and Sigourney Weaver; *Indiana Jones and the Temple of Doom* starring Harrison Ford; *Police Academy* starring Steve Guttenberg; *Gremlins* starring Phoebe Cates; and *Footloose* starring Kevin Bacon. Johnny Depp, Charlie Sheen, Marisa Tomei, Val Kilmer, John Malkovich, and Tim Roth made their film debuts. TV show premieres included *The Cosby Show; Miami Vice; Night Court; Who's the Boss?; Murder, She Wrote; Hunter;* and *Punky Brewster*.

INDUSTRY: Steve Jobs introduced Apple's Macintosh personal computer (the first PC to use a mouse). Mac's famous '1984' TV commercial appeared only once, during Super Bowl XVIII. Parker Brothers sold over 20 million units of the board game Trivial Pursuit.

LITERATURE: Works published include Tom Clancy's *The Hunt for Red October;* John Updike's *The Witches of Eastwick;* Gore Vidal's *Lincoln;* and Stephen King's *Thinner* and *The Talisman*.

MUSIC: The Police's "Every Breath You Take" won the Song of the Year Grammy Award. Culture Club won Best New Artist. Other top songs were Cyndi Lauper's "Girls Just Wanna Have Fun" and "Time After Time;" Prince's "Purple Rain" and "When Doves Cry;" Bruce Springsteen's "Born in the U.S.A.;" The Cars' "Drive;" and "Careless Whisper" by Wham! Dan Aykroyd and Bette Midler hosted the first MTV Video Music Awards that featured Madonna's classic performance of "Like a Virgin." Marvin Gaye was shot and killed by his father during an argument.

SPORTS: Baseball: The AL's Detroit Tigers defeated the NL's San Diego Padres 4 games to 1 in the World Series. Football: The Los Angeles Raiders beat the Washington Redskins 38-9 in Super Bowl XVIII. Team USA won the most medals (174) and the most gold medals (83) at the Summer Olympics in Los Angeles.

THEATRE: David Mamet's Broadway play *Glengarry Glen Ross* won the Pulitzer Prize for Drama. Stephen Sondheim's Broadway musical *Sunday in the Park with George* won the Pulitzer Prize for Musical Drama.

1985

BIRTHS: Racecar driver Kyle Busch (May 2) holds the NASCAR records for most race wins in a season (24 in 2010) and the most career Nationwide Series wins with 51. Model Kendra Wilkinson (June 12) was one of Hugh Hefner's 3 girlfriends, and her life in the Playboy Mansion was documented on the reality TV series *The Girls Next Door*. Michael Phelps (June 30) is a retired swimmer who has won 22 Olympic medals, 18 of which are gold medals. Both are all time record totals, more than any other Olympic athlete. Sprinter Allyson Felix (November 18) has won 4 Olympic and World Championship gold medals in the women's 200-meter race.

ART & ARCHITECTURE: The Strawberry Fields Memorial is a 2.5-acre section of Central Park in New York City that is dedicated to the memory of musician and former Beatle John Lennon. Pop artist Andy Warhol created the 'Portrait of Seymour H. Knox' in his famous duplicative, multicolored style. The 72-story, 921-foot tall Bank of America is the tallest building in Dallas, Texas. The skyscraper's outline is accented by neon green argon lighting along all of its edges.

FILM & TV: *Out of Africa* won the Best Picture Academy Award and the Best Director Oscar for Sydney Pollack. Other top films were *Back to the Future* starring Michael J. Fox and Christopher Lloyd; *The Color Purple* starring Whoopi Goldberg and Danny Glover; *Cocoon* starring Don Ameche and Wilford Brimley; *The Jewel of the Nile* starring Michael Douglas and Kathleen Turner; and *Witness* starring Harrison Ford and Kelly McGillis. Ethan Hawke, Joan Allen, Viggo Mortensen, Stanley Tucci, and River Phoenix made their film debuts. TV show premieres included *The Golden Girls; Moonlighting; Growing Pains; Mr. Belvedere; Larry King Live;* and *MacGyver*.

INDUSTRY: Coca-Cola introduced New Coke, which turned into a major marketing failure, resulting in the reintroduction of Coke's original recipe under the name Coca-Cola Classic. The first Blockbuster Video Rental store opened in Dallas, Texas. Samuel Adams Boston Lager was voted 'Best Beer in America' at the Great American Beer Festival, beating out 93 other beers.

LITERATURE: Works published include Larry McMurtry's *Lonesome Dove;* Garrison Keillor's *Lake Wobegon Days;* John Irving's *The Cider House Rules;* Anne Tyler's *The Accidental Tourist;* Gabriel Garcia Marquez's *Love in the Time of Cholera;* and Priscilla Presley's *Elvis and Me*.

MUSIC: Tina Turner's "What's Love Got to Do with It" won the Song of the Year Grammy Award. Cyndi Lauper won Best New Artist. Other top songs were John Fogerty's "Centerfield," Glenn Frey's "The Heat Is On," a-ha's "Take On Me," Foreigner's "I Want to Know What Love Is," and Dire Straits' "Money for Nothing." The Live Aid concert was held in London and Philadelphia to raise relief funds for Ethiopian Famine. The first Farm Aid concert was held in Champaign, Illinois.

SPORTS: Baseball: The AL's Kansas City Royals defeated the NL's St. Louis Cardinals 4 games to 3 in the World Series. Pete Rose of the Cincinnati Reds broke Ty Cobb's career record of 4,191 hits. Football: The San Francisco 49ers beat the Miami Dolphins 38-16 in Super Bowl XIX. Libby Riddles became the first woman to win the Iditarod Sled Dog Race, with her lead dogs Axle and Dugan.

THEATRE: Neil Simon's semi-autobiographical Broadway play *Biloxi Blues* starred Matthew Broderick and won the Tony Award for Best Play.

1986

BIRTHS: Singer-songwriter Lady Gaga (March 28) has won 5 Grammy awards and 13 MTV Video Music Awards. In 2011, she was named the 4th best selling digital artist of all time in the U.S. with total digital sales of over 42 million singles. Professional football player Michael Oher (May 28) plays offensive tackle for the NFL's Baltimore Ravens. His turbulent upbringing and subsequent rise to success are detailed in the 2009 Academy Award winning film *The Blind Side*. Mary Kate and Ashley Olsen (June 13) are acting twins who began their career as infants on the TV series *Full House*. They have amassed a fortune of more than $100 million through the sale of their own branded clothing, movies, fragrances, books, and magazines. Shaun White (September 3) is a professional snowboarder who has won 2 Olympic gold medals and 12 Winter X Games gold medals.

ART: Andy Warhol created his *Camouflage Self-Portrait* a few months before his death. It is currently displayed at New York City's Metropolitan Museum of Art. Sculptor Robert Graham produced the Monument to Joe Louis, a 24-foot-long arm with a fisted hand suspended by a 24-foot-high pyramid framework that stands outside Hart Plaza in Detroit, Michigan.

FILM & TV: *Platoon* won the best Picture Academy Award and the Best Director Oscar for Oliver Stone. Other top films were *Crocodile Dundee* starring Paul Hogan; *Top Gun* starring Tom Cruise and Kelly McGillis; *Aliens* starring Sigourney Weaver; *The Golden Child* starring Eddie Murphy; *Ferris Bueller's Day Off* starring Matthew Broderick; *Stand by Me* starring River Phoenix and Wil Wheaton; and *Back to School* starring Rodney Dangerfield. Kevin Spacey, Marlee Matlin, Woody Harrelson, and Angela Bassett made their film debuts. TV show premieres included *L.A. Law; Perfect Strangers; Head of the Class; Matlock; ALF;* and *Pee-wee's Playhouse*.

INDUSTRY: NASA's Space Shuttle *Challenger* disintegrated 73 seconds after the launch of its 10th mission, killing all 7 crew members. The largest U.S. pet supply company, PetSmart, was founded in Phoenix, Arizona offering grooming services and pet hotel facilities.

MUSIC: USA for Africa's "We Are the World" won the Song of the Year Grammy Award. Sade won Best New Artist. Other top songs were Madonna's "Papa Don't Preach;" Europe's "The Final Countdown;" The Pet Shop Boys' "West End Girls;" Bon Jovi's "Livin' On a Prayer;" The Jets' "Crush on You;" Robert Palmer's "Addicted to Love;" and Berlin's "Take My Breath Away." Elvis Presley, Chuck Berry, Little Richard, Ray Charles, Fats Domino, James Brown, The Everly Brothers, Jerry Lee Lewis, and Buddy Holly became the first inductees into the Rock and Roll Hall of Fame in Cleveland, Ohio.

SPORTS: Baseball: The NL's New York Mets defeated the AL's Boston Red Sox 4 games to 3 in the World Series. Football: The Chicago Bears beat the New England Patriots 46-10 in Super Bowl XX. The Pennsylvania State University Nittany Lions were college football national champions with a 12-0 record. Boxing: Mike Tyson knocked out Trevor Berbick in the 2nd round to become the youngest World Heavyweight Champion at the age of 20 years and 4 months. Golf: Jack Nicklaus won the last of his 18 major golf championship titles and became the oldest player to win the Masters Tournament at the age of 46. Cycling: Greg LeMond became the first U.S. winner of the Tour de France.

1987

BIRTHS: Kesha (March 1) is a singer-songwriter whose 2010 album *Animal* debuted at number 1 in the U.S. and produced 2 chart-topping singles: "Tik Tok," and "We R Who We R." Pro football player Tim Tebow (August 14) plays quarterback for the New York Jets. He won the 2007 Heisman Trophy at the University of Florida and led the Gators to 2 national championships, in 2006 and 2008. Actor Zac Efron (October 18) is best known for starring in the Disney film trilogy *High School Musical* and the 2007 film version of the Broadway musical *Hairspray.* Swimmer Dana Vollmer (November 13) has won a total of 30 medals in major international competition, including the gold medal at the 2012 London Olympics where she set the world record in the women's 100-meter butterfly event at 55.98 seconds.

FILM & TV: *The Last Emperor* won the Best Picture Academy Award and the Best Director Oscar for Bernardo Bertolucci. Other top films were *Moonstruck* starring Cher (Best Actress Oscar) and Nicolas Cage; *Three Men and a Baby* starring Tom Selleck, Ted Danson, and Steve Guttenberg; *Fatal Attraction* starring Michael Douglas and Glenn Close; *Dirty Dancing* starring Patrick Swayze and Jennifer Grey; *Lethal Weapon* starring Mel Gibson and Danny Glover; and *Good Morning, Vietnam* starring Robin Williams. Brad Pitt, Alec Baldwin, George Clooney, Sandra Bullock, Chris Rock, and Ben Stiller made their film debuts. TV show premieres included *Married... with Children; Full House; 21 Jump Street; The Tracy Ullman Show; Jake and the Fatman; Thirtysomething; Star Trek: The Next Generation;* and *A Different World.*

INDUSTRY: Director Rob Reiner named his film and TV production company Castle Rock Entertainment for the fictional Maine town used in many Stephen King novels (named by King from the fictional Castle Rock in the novel *Lord of the Flies*). The J. Peterman Company sells clothing and fashion accessories mainly through catalogs. The 1990s TV series *Seinfeld* parodied the owner with a catalog-company businessman named J. Peterman.

MUSIC: Dionne Warwick's "That's What Friends Are For" won the Song of the Year. Bruce Hornsby and the Range won Best New Artist. Other top songs were Los Lobos' "La Bamba;" Michael Jackson's "Bad;" Bon Jovi's "Wanted Dead or Alive;" Suzanne Vega's "Luka;" Aerosmith's "Rag Doll;" Gun N' Roses' "Sweet Child o' Mine;" U2's "With or Without You;" and The Grateful Dead's "Touch of Grey." Aretha Franklin became the first woman inducted into the Rock and Roll Hall of Fame, along with Smokey Robinson, Bo Diddley, Jackie Wilson, Roy Orbison, Eddie Cochran, The Coasters, Marvin Gaye, Carl Perkins, Ricky Nelson, Bill Haley, and Clyde McPhatter.

SPORTS: Baseball: The AL's Minnesota Twins defeated the NL's St. Louis Cardinals 4 games to 3 in the World Series. Football: The New York Giants beat the Denver Broncos 39-20 in Super Bowl XXI. Basketball: The Los Angeles Lakers defeated the Boston Celtic 4 games to 2 in the NBA Finals. The Indiana University Hoosiers beat the Syracuse University Orangemen 74-73 to win the NCAA men's basketball tournament. Yacht Racing: USA's *Stars & Stripes '87* defeated Australia's defending champion *Kookaburra III* to capture the America's Cup in San Diego Bay, California.

THEATRE: Alfred Uhry's Pulitzer Prize winning play *Driving Miss Daisy* starred Dana Ivey and Morgan Freeman and ran for 1,195 performances.

1988

BIRTHS: Actor Haley Joel Osment (April 10) portrayed the son of Tom Hanks' title character in the 1994 film *Forrest Gump,* but he is best known for his performance as Cole Sear in the 1999 thriller film *The Sixth Sense.*
Professional baseball player Stephen Strasburg (July 20) is a pitcher for Major League Baseball's Washington Nationals. He set a Nationals franchise record with 14 strikeouts in his 2010 major league debut. Pro basketball player Jeremy Lin (August 23) created a global following known as *Linsanity* by unexpectedly leading the National Basketball Association's New York Knicks during the 2011-12 season. Kevin Durant (September 29) plays pro basketball for the NBA's Oklahoma City Thunder. In 2010 he became the youngest player ever to win the NBA scoring title.

FILM & TV: *Rain Man* won the Best Picture Academy Award as well as the Best Director Oscar for Barry Levinson and the Best Actor Oscar for Dustin Hoffman. Other top films were *Big* starring Tom Hanks and Elizabeth Perkins; *Twins* starring Arnold Schwarzenegger and Danny DeVito; *Die Hard* starring Bruce Willis and Alan Rickman; *A Fish Called Wanda* starring John Cleese and Jamie Lee Curtis; *Who Framed Roger Rabbit* starring Bob Hoskins and Kathleen Turner; *Coming to America* starring Eddie Murphy and Arsenio Hall; and *The Naked Gun* starring Leslie Nielsen. Matt Damon, Gary Sinise, Annette Bening, Steven Seagal, and Uma Thurman made their film debuts. TV show premieres included *The Wonder Years; America's Most Wanted; Roseanne; Empty Nest;* and *Murphy Brown.*

INDUSTRY: The Chrysler Corporation formed the Eagle car division with their buyout of American Motors. Popular Eagle car models included the Premier, Summit, and Talon. The Upper Deck sports trading card company was founded in Yorba Linda, California with baseball player Ken Griffey, Jr. as their first card ever produced. XM Satellite Radio started as the American Mobile Satellite Corporation, broadcasting telephone, fax, and data signals.

MUSIC: Linda Ronstadt and James Ingram's "Somewhere Out There" won the Song of the Year Grammy award. Jody Watley won Best New Artist. Other top songs were Living Colour's "Cult of Personality;" Belinda Carlisle's "Heaven is a Place on Earth;" Poison's "Every Rose Has Its Thorn;" Tracy Chapman's "Fast Car;" and The Beach Boys' "Kokomo." John Fogerty won a self-plagiarism lawsuit with Fantasy records. The record label claimed that Fogerty's 1985 comeback hit "The Old Man Down the Road" was too similar to his 1970 Creedence Clearwater Revival song "Run Through the Jungle."

SPORTS: Baseball: The NL's Los Angeles Dodgers defeated the AL's Oakland Athletics 4 games to 1 in the World Series. Football: The Washington Redskins beat the Denver Broncos 42-10 in Super Bowl XXII. The University of Notre Dame Fighting Irish were college football national champions with a 12-0 record. Basketball: The Los Angeles Lakers defeated the Detroit Pistons 4 games to 3 in the NBA Finals. The Kansas Jayhawks beat the Oklahoma Sooners 83-79 to win the NCAA men's basketball tournament.

THEATRE: Andrew Lloyd Webber's musical *The Phantom of the Opera* won the Tony Award for Best Musical and is the most successful entertainment project in history, setting Broadway records for box office receipts at $845 million. It is the longest running show in Broadway history, currently in its 24th year with over 10,000 performances.

1989

BIRTHS: Singer Chris Brown (May 5) was the first male solo artist to have his debut single, 2005's "Run It!," reach number 1 since Diddy in 1997. Alex Morgan (July 2) plays forward for the Seattle Sounders Women soccer team. She won a goal medal at the 2012 London Olympics when she became the youngest U.S. player to score 20 goals in one season. Professional golfer Michelle Wie (October 11) became the youngest player to qualify for a United States Golf Association amateur championship at age 10. She turned professional in 2005 at age 15. Singer-songwriter Taylor Swift (December 13) became the youngest person to write and perform a number one song on the country music chart (2006's "Our Song" at age 16).

ART & ARCHITECTURE: The Minneapolis Institute of Art exhibited *Jim Dine Drawings 1973-1987*, featuring works by the Pop Art pioneer. Los Angeles' 73-story, 1,018-foot tall U.S. Bank Tower is the tallest building in California and the tallest in the world with a rooftop heliport. The I.M. Pei designed Morton H. Meyerson Symphony Center in Dallas, Texas, is considered one of the world's greatest orchestra halls.

FILM & TV: *Driving Miss Daisy* won the Best Picture Academy Award and the Best Actress Oscar for Jessica Tandy. Other top films were *Batman* starring Michael Keaton and Jack Nicholson; *Dead Poets Society* starring Robin Williams and Ethan Hawke; *Born on the Fourth of July* starring Tom Cruise and Willem Dafoe; *Look Who's Talking* starring John Travolta and Kirstie Alley; *Honey, I Shrunk the Kids* starring Rick Moranis and Marcia Strassman; and Disney's *The Little Mermaid*. Adam Sandler, Rene Russo, John C. Reilly, Tom Sizemore, and Rosie Perez made their film debuts. TV show premieres included *Seinfeld; Coach; The Simpsons; Saved by the Bell; Doogie Howser, M.D.; Baywatch; COPS;* and *Quantum Leap.*

INDUSTRY: Donna Karan founded her own fashion brand, DKNY, in New York City. Compaq introduced the first laptop computer, the LTE 286, which came with 40 megabytes of memory and sold for $5,399.

MUSIC: Bobby McFerrin's "Don't Worry, Be Happy" won the Song of the Year Grammy award. Tracy Chapman won Best New Artist. Other top songs were The Bangles' "Eternal Flame;" Madonna's "Like a Prayer;" Chicago's "Look Away;" Bobby Brown's "My Prerogative;" The B-52's' "Love Shack;" Paula Abdul's "Straight Up;" Richard Marx's "Right Here Waiting;" and Janet Jackson's "Miss You Much." Madonna filed for divorce from actor Sean Penn after nearly 4 years of marriage, citing irreconcilable differences.

SPORTS: Baseball: The AL's Oakland Athletics swept the NL's San Francisco Giants 4 games to 0 in the World Series, best remembered for the Loma Prieta earthquake that struck just before game 3 was due to begin. Pete Rose was banned for life from baseball following accusations that he gambled on baseball games while playing for and managing the Cincinnati Reds. Football: The San Francisco 49ers defeated the Cincinnati Bengals 20-16 in Super Bowl XXIII. The Miami Hurricanes won their 3rd college football national championship of the decade. Basketball: The Detroit Pistons swept The Los Angeles Lakers 4 games to 0 to win their first NBA Finals championship. The Michigan Wolverines beat the Seton Hall Pirates 80-79 in overtime to win the NCAA men's basketball tournament.

1990

On April 1, the U.S. population was 248,709,873 people. The average yearly income for a U.S. worker was $21,028, equal to $35,203 today; the average house cost $122,900, equal to $205,745 today; the average car cost $11,300, equal to $18,917 today; a gallon of gas cost $1.16, equal to $1.94 today; and a gallon of milk cost $1.42, equal to $2.37 today.

BIRTHS: Actress Kristen Stewart (April 9) stars in *the Twilight Saga* film series and became Hollywood's highest paid actress in 2012. Racecar driver Joey Logano (May 24) became the youngest driver to ever win a NASCAR racing event at age 18 in 2008. Rapper Soulja Boy (July 28) is best known for his 2007 hit single "Crank That (Soulja Boy)," which stayed at number-one for 7 weeks. Jamie Anderson (September 13) is a female professional snowboarder who has won 3 Gold Medals at the X Games in Aspen, Colorado since 2007.

ART: Two thieves dressed as police officers stole 13 paintings worth an estimated $500 million from the Isabella Gardner Museum in Boston, Massachusetts. The stolen pieces by such artists as Rembrandt, Manet, Vermeer, and Degas have yet to be recovered. It is the largest single property theft in recorded history.

FILM & TV: *Dances with Wolves* won the Best Picture Academy Award and the Best Director Oscar for Kevin Costner. Other top films were *Home Alone* starring Macauley Culkin, Joe Pesci, and Daniel Stern; *Ghost* starring Patrick Swayze, Demi Moore, and Whoopi Goldberg (Best Supporting Actress Oscar); *Pretty Woman* starring Julia Roberts and Richard Gere; and *Total Recall* starring Arnold Schwarzenegger. Russell Crowe, Julianne Moore, Chris O'Donnell, Hank Azaria, and Catherine Zeta-Jones made their film debuts. TV show premieres included *Twin Peaks; In Living Color; Northern Exposure; The Fresh Prince of Bel-Air; Wings; Beverly Hills, 90210;* and *Law & Order.*

INDUSTRY: Lucky Brand Jeans, a designer denim company and subsidiary of Liz Claiborne fashions, was founded in Vernon, California. SkyMall is an in-flight product catalog that is distributed in airplane seat pockets and is read by more than 650 million air travelers annually. Universal Studios Florida was founded in Orlando and is the 8th most visited U.S. theme park.

MUSIC: Bette Midler's "Wind Beneath My Wings" won the Song of the Year Grammy Award. Milli Vanilli's Best New Artist Award was revoked when it was revealed that they did not perform on their record. Other top songs were Madonna's "Vogue," Alannah Miles' "Black Velvet," and Vanilla Ice's "Ice Ice Baby." 35-year-old guitarist Stevie Ray Vaughan died in a helicopter crash at Alpine Valley Music Theatre in East Troy, Wisconsin on August 27.

SPORTS: Baseball: The NL's Cincinnati Reds swept the AL's Oakland Athletics 4 games to 0 in the World Series. Football: The San Francisco 49ers beat the Denver Broncos 55-10 in Super Bowl XXIV. Boxing: Buster Douglas defeated Mike Tyson with a 10th round knockout to win the World Heavyweight Title in what many consider the biggest upset in boxing history. Dogsled Racing: Susan Butcher won her 4th and final Iditarod Sled Dog Race with her lead dogs Sluggo and Lightning.

1991

BIRTHS: Actress Emma Roberts (February 10) is the daughter of actor Eric Roberts and the niece of actress Julia Roberts. She is best known for her role as Addie Singer in the Nickelodeon TV series *Unfabulous*. Musician Wolfgang Van Halen (March 16) is the son of Eddie Van Halen and Valerie Bertinelli. He plays bass alongside his father in the rock band Van Halen. Derrick Williams (May 25) is a forward for the National Basketball Association's Minnesota Timberwolves. He was the Timberwolves highest draft selection in franchise history, being picked #2 overall in the 2011 NBA Draft. Erik Per Sullivan (July 12) is an actor best known for portraying the youngest son Dewey on the Fox TV series *Malcolm in the Middle* for 6 seasons.

ART & ARCHITECTURE: The Space Mirror Memorial is dedicated to the lives of the 20 men and women of NASA who have died in various U.S. space programs. It is located on the grounds of the John F. Kennedy Space Center on Merritt Island, Florida. Designed by architect Cesar Pelli, the 57-story, 947-foot tall Key Tower in Cleveland is the tallest building in Ohio.

FILM & TV: *The Silence of the Lambs* was the 3rd film to win Oscars in all top 5 categories: Best Picture, Best Director (Jonathan Demme), Best Actor (Anthony Hopkins), Best Actress (Jodie Foster), and Best Screenplay (Ted Tally). Other top films were *Hook* starring Dustin Hoffman, Robin Williams, and Julia Roberts; *Robin Hood: Prince of Thieves* starring Kevin Costner and Morgan Freeman; *Cape Fear* starring Robert De Niro and Nick Nolte; *JFK* starring Kevin Costner, Tommy Lee Jones, and Gary Oldman; *City Slickers* starring Billy Crystal and Jack Palance; and Disney's *Beauty and the Beast*. Halle Berry, Leonardo DiCaprio, Gwynyth Paltrow, Philip Seymour Hoffman, and Reese Witherspoon made their film debuts. TV show premieres included *Home Improvement; Blossom; The Ren & Stimpy Show;* and *Rugrats*.

LITERATURE: Douglas Coupland's novel *Generation X: Tales for an Accelerated Culture* popularized the term Generation X as the name for the birth period from the early 1960s to the early 1980s.

MUSIC: Bette Midler's "From a Distance" won the Song of the Year Grammy Award. Mariah Carey won the Best New Artist. Other top songs were R.E.M.'s "Losing My Religion;" Michael Jackson's "Black Or White;" Scorpions' "Wind of Change;" Lenny Kravitz' "Always on the Run;" Prince's "Cream;" Metallica's "Enter Sandman;" Pearl Jam's "Jeremy;" Bonnie Raitt's "I Can't Make You Love Me;" Soundgarden's "Outshined;" and Red Hot Chili Peppers' "Under the Bridge." Nirvana released their 2nd album, *Nevermind,* which helped establish the popularity of Grunge music worldwide.

SPORTS: Baseball: The AL's Minnesota Twins defeated the NL's Atlanta Braves 4 games to 3 in the World Series. With 69 innings in total, it holds the record for the longest 7 game World Series ever. Football: The New York Giants beat the Buffalo Bills 20-19 in Super Bowl XXV. Basketball: The Chicago Bulls defeated the Los Angeles Lakers 4 games to 1 to win Chicago's first NBA title, starting a run of 6 titles in 8 seasons. Hockey: The Pittsburgh Penguins beat the Minnesota North Stars 4 games to 2 to win the Stanley Cup. Motor Racing: Rick Mears won the Indianapolis 500, becoming the third driver to win the race 4 times.

THEATRE: Neil Simon's Broadway play *Lost in Yonkers* won the Pulitzer Prize for Drama and starred Kevin Spacey and Mercedes Ruehl.

1992

BIRTHS: Gymnast Shawn Johnson (January 19) won the 2008 Olympic balance beam Gold Medal and in 2009 she was the winner of TV's *Dancing with the Stars.* Actor Taylor Lautner (February 11) stars in *The Twilight Saga* film series and in 2010 he became the highest paid teenage actor in Hollywood. Frances Bean Cobain (August 18) is the only child of rock musicians Kurt Cobain and Courtney Love. Her godparents are R.E.M. singer Michael Stipe and actress Drew Barrymore. Actress and singer Miley Cyrus (November 23) first gained fame for starring as the title role in the Disney Channel's sitcom *Hannah Montana.* Her father is country music singer Billy Ray Cyrus.

ARCHITECTURE: Atlanta's 55-story, 1,040-foot tall Bank of America Plaza is the tallest building in Georgia and the tallest building in the U.S. outside of Chicago and New York City. Also located in Atlanta, Georgia, is the Georgia Dome. With a capacity of 71,288, it is home to the NFL's Atlanta Falcons.

FILM & TV: *Unforgiven* won the Best Picture Academy Award as well as the Best Director Oscar for Clint Eastwood and the Best Supporting Actor Oscar for Gene Hackman. Other top films were *The Bodyguard* starring Kevin Costner and Whitney Houston; *Basic Instinct* starring Michael Douglas and Sharon Stone; *A Few Good Men* starring Tom Cruise and Demi Moore; *Wayne's World* starring Mike Myers and Dana Carvey; and *Sister Act* starring Whoopi Goldberg. Will Smith, Gary Sinise, Laura Linney, Ralph Fiennes, Hillary Swank, Jamie Foxx, and Heath Ledger made their film debuts. TV show premieres included *Melrose Place; Barney & Friends; Dateline NBC; The Real World; Picket Fences;* and *The Tonight Show with Jay Leno.*

INDUSTRY: Dan Aykroyd, star of The Blues Brothers band and films, founded the House of Blues chain of live music concert halls and restaurants. Locations include Chicago, New Orleans, Boston, Dallas, and Las Vegas.

LITERATURE: Relationship counselor John Gray's *Men Are from Mars, Women Are from Venus* was the highest ranked nonfiction work of the 1990s, selling over 7 million copies. It spent 121 weeks on the bestseller list. Other works published include John Grisham's *The Pelican Brief;* Terry McMillan's *Waiting to Exhale;* Stephen King's *Dolores Claiborne;* Toni Morrison's *Jazz;* and Robert James Waller's *The Bridges of Madison County.*

MUSIC: "Unforgettable," a duet performed by Natalie Cole with her father Nat King Cole, won the Song of the Year Grammy Award. Marc Cohn won Best New Artist. Other top songs were Boyz II Men's "End of the Road;" Whitney Houston's "I Will Always Love You;" Nirvana's "Smells Like Teen Spirit;" Mr. Big's "To Be With You;" Sir Mix-a-Lot's "Baby Got Back;" and R.E.M.'s "Drive." Guns N' Roses' "November Rain" at 8 minutes, 57 seconds, set the world's record for being the longest single to reach the U.S. Top 20.

SPORTS: Baseball: The AL's Toronto Blue Jays defeated the NL's Atlanta Braves 4 games to 2 in the first World Series won by a Canadian team. Football: The Washington Redskins beat the Buffalo Bills 37-24 in Super Bowl XXVI. Hockey: The Pittsburgh Penguins swept the Chicago Blackhawks 4 games to 0 to win the Stanley Cup. Boxing: Oscar De La Hoya won a gold medal at the Barcelona Olympics, earning him the nickname 'Golden Boy.'

1993

BIRTHS: Bobbi Kristina Houston Brown (March 4) is the daughter of singers Whitney Houston and Bobby Brown. Actress Miranda Cosgrove (May 14) stars as Carly Shay on the Nickelodeon TV series *iCarly,* for which she became the highest paid child star on TV, making $180,000 per episode. Scotty McCreery (October 9) is a singer who won the 10th season of Fox TV's *American Idol.* His debut album, *Clear as Day,* has sold over 1 million copies and spawned two top 20 country songs: "I Love You This Big" and "The Trouble with Girls." Motorcycle racer Elena Myers (November 21) became the first woman to win a professional motorsports race of any kind at Florida's Daytona International Speedway on March 17, 2012.

ART: The Vietnam Women's Memorial on the National Mall in Washington D.C. is dedicated to the U.S. women who served in the Vietnam War, most of whom were nurses.

FILM & TV: *Schindler's List* won the Best Picture Academy Award and the Best Director Oscar for Steven Spielberg. Other top films were *Jurassic Park* starring Sam Neill, Laura Dern, and Jeff Goldblum; *Mrs. Doubtfire* starring Robin Williams and Sally Field; *The Fugitive* starring Harrison Ford and Tommy Lee Jones (Best Supporting Actor Oscar); *The Firm* starring Tom Cruise and Gene Hackman; and *Philadelphia* starring Tom Hanks (Best Actor Oscar) and Denzel Washington. Actor River Phoenix died from an overdose of heroin and cocaine outside The Viper Room nightclub (owned by Johnny Depp) in Hollywood, California. Matthew McConaughey, Jennifer Aniston, Terrance Howard, Mira Sorvino, Vince Vaughn, and Kate Beckinsale made their film debuts. TV show premieres included *The X-Files; NYPD Blue; The Nanny; Frasier; Late Night with Conan O'Brien;* and *Walker, Texas Ranger.*

INDUSTRY: Taser International manufactures the Taser non-lethal electroshock gun. TASER takes its name from a fictional weapon: Thomas A. Swift's Electric Rifle. Chipotle Mexican Grill, a chain of Mexican food restaurants, was founded in Denver, Colorado. A chipotle is the Spanish name for a smoked and dried jalapeno chili pepper.

MUSIC: Eric Clapton's "Tears in Heaven" won the Song of the Year Grammy Award. Arrested Development won Best New Artist. Other top songs were Lenny Kravitz' "Are You Gonna Go My Way;" Gin Blossoms' "Hey Jealousy;" Mariah Carey's "Hero;" The Smashing Pumpkins' "Disarm;" Aerosmith's "Livin' on the Edge;" and Soul Asylum's "Runaway Train." Musician Prince changed his name to an unpronounceable symbol on his 35th birthday, which led to him being called 'The Artist Formerly Known as Prince.'

SPORTS: Baseball: The AL's Toronto Blue Jays outfielder Joe Carter hit the 2nd ever walk-off home run to win a World Series, in game 6 over the NL's Philadelphia Phillies. Football: The Dallas Cowboys beat the Buffalo Bills 52-17 to win Super Bowl XXVII. Mixed Martial Arts: The first Ultimate Fighting Championship (UFC 1) was held in front of 2,800 people at McNichols Arena in Denver, Colorado, with another 86,000 watching on Pay Per View TV. Royce Gracie of Brazil defeated Gerard Gordeau of the Netherlands by submission in the final match.

THEATRE: *The Who's Tommy,* the Broadway musical based on Pete Townshend's 1969 rock opera album *Tommy,* ran for 899 performances and won 5 Tony Awards from 11 nominations.

1994

BIRTHS: Actress Dakota Fanning (February 23) has appeared in such films as *I Am Sam* (for which she became the youngest person ever to be nominated for a Screen Actors Guild Award in 2002), *War of the Worlds, Man on Fire, Charlotte's Web,* and *The Runaways.* Akiane Kramarik (July 9) is a self-taught painter and poet who started painting at the age of 6 and began writing poetry at the age of 7. Her first self-portrait painting sold for $10,000. Actor Mark Indelicato (July 16) is best known for his role as Justin Suarez, the fashion-obsessed nephew of Betty Suarez, on the ABC TV series *Ugly Betty* from 2006 to 2010. Professional skateboarder Nyjah Huston (November 30) has won 4 medals, including 1 gold medal at the Summer X Games in Los Angeles, California.

ART: Married sculptors Omri Amrany and Julie Rotblatt-Amrany created the 12-foot tall bronze and granite statue *The Spirit,* which depicts legendary Chicago Bulls basketball player Michael Jordan and stands outside Chicago, Illinois' United Center.

FILM & TV: *Forrest Gump* won the Best Picture Academy Award as well as the Best Director Oscar for Robert Zemeckis and the Best Actor Oscar for Tom Hanks. Other top films were *True Lies* starring Arnold Schwarzenegger and Jamie Lee Curtis; *The Mask* starring Jim Carrey and Cameron Diaz; *Speed* starring Keanu Reeves and Sandra Bullock; *Interview with a Vampire* starring Tom Cruise and Brad Pitt; and Disney's *The Lion King.* Chris Tucker, Natalie Portman, Mark Wahlberg, Kate Winslet, Jude Law, and Michelle Williams made their film debuts. TV show premieres included *Friends; ER; Party of Five; Chicago Hope; My So Called Life;* and *Ellen.*

INDUSTRY: Media moguls Steven Spielberg, Jaffrey Katzenberg, and David Geffen founded DreamWorks film studio, which won 3 consecutive Best Picture Academy Awards with 1999's *American Beauty,* 2000's *Gladiator,* and 2001's *A Beautiful Mind.* Sky Dayton started the network provider company EarthLink at the age of 23 after spending an entire week trying to configure his computer for Internet access.

MUSIC: Peebo Bryson and Regina Belle's "A Whole New World (Aladdin's Theme)" won the Song of the Year Grammy Award. Toni Braxton won Best New Artist. Other top songs were Sheryl Crow's "All I Wanna Do;" Mariah Carey's "Without You;" All-4-One's "I Swear;" and Beastie Boys' "Sabotage." 350,000 people attended Woodstock '94, a music festival celebrating the 25th anniversary of the original 1969 Woodstock Festival, in Saugerties, New York. Nirvana's singer and guitarist Kurt Cobain died from a self-inflicted shotgun wound to the head at his home in Seattle, Washington.

SPORTS: Baseball: The World Series was cancelled for the first time since 1904, due to a labor strike by Major League Baseball players. Football: The Dallas Cowboys beat the Buffalo Bills 30-13 in Super Bowl XXVIII. Hockey: The New York Rangers defeated the Vancouver Canucks 4 games to 3 to win the Stanley Cup. Boxing: 45-year-old George Foreman became the oldest Heavyweight Champion in boxing history when he knocked out Michael Moorer in the 10th round of a Las Vegas fight.

THEATRE: The Broadway musical *Beauty and the Beast* ran for 13 years and 5,464 performances. It has played in 13 countries and 115 cities worldwide, grossing more than $1.4 billion.

1995

BIRTHS: Hailey Clauson (March 7) is a fashion model who has been the face of Gucci, Forever 21, and Jill Stuart. She also appeared in the 2009 music video for rapper Jay-Z's *Empire State of Mind*. Swimmer Missy Franklin (May 10) is a 4-time Olympic gold medal winner and the current world record holder in the women's 200-meter backstroke. Tommy Batchelor (August 23) is a dancer who performed in 2 productions of *The Nutcracker* ballet and starred in the title role of the 2009 Broadway musical *Billy Elliot*. Gymnast McKayla Maroney (December 9) was a member of the gold medal-winning U.S. Women's Gymnastics team at the 2012 London Olympics.

ART: The Korean War Veterans Memorial on the National Mall in Washington D.C. features 19 stainless steel statues of U.S. armed forces soldiers. There appear to be 38 soldiers when reflected on the Memorial's wall, representing the 38th parallel, the demarcation line between North and South Korea. The daily comic strip *Calvin and Hobbes*, written and illustrated by Bill Watterson, ended after 10 years of syndication.

FILM & TV: *Braveheart* won the Best Picture Academy Award and the Best Director Oscar for Mel Gibson. Other top films were *Batman Forever* starring Val Kilmer and Tommy Lee Jones; *Die Hard with a Vengeance* starring Bruce Willis and Samuel L. Jackson; *Seven* starring Brad Pitt and Morgan Freeman; *Waterworld* starring Kevin Costner and Dennis Hopper; *Apollo 13* starring Tom Hanks; and Disney's *Toy Story*. Michael Clarke Duncan, Charlize Theron, Jeremy Renner, Chloe Sevigny, and Paul Rudd made their film debuts. TV show premieres included *NewsRadio*; *The Drew Carey Show*; *MADtv*; *JAG*; *Caroline in the City*; *Star Trek: Voyager*; and *Ned & Stacey*.

INDUSTRY: Amazon.com was founded in Seattle, Washington and is now the world's largest online retailer with 2011 revenues of $48.07 billion. Yahoo! Internet web portal attracts 700 million computer users every month. One of the first items sold on the eBay online auction website was a broken laser pointer for $14.83.

LITERATURE: Works published include Michael Crichton's *The Lost World*; Nick Hornby's *High Fidelity*; John Grisham's *The Rainmaker*; Frank McCourt's *Angela's Ashes*; and Leonard Nimoy's autobiography, *I Am Spock*.

MUSIC: Bruce Springsteen's "Streets of Philadelphia" won the Song of the Year Grammy Award. Sheryl Crow won Best New Artist. Other top songs were Coolio's "Gangsta's Paradise;" Weezer's "Buddy Holly;" No Doubt's "Just a Girl;" Goo Goo Dolls' "Name;" and Blues Traveler's "Run-Around." 53-year-old Grateful Dead guitarist Jerry Garcia died in his sleep from a heart attack at Serenity Knolls rehab facility in Forest Knolls, California.

SPORTS: Baseball: The NL's Atlanta Braves defeated the AL's Cleveland Indians 4 games to 2 in the World Series. Baltimore Oriole shortstop Cal Ripken broke Lou Gehrig's MLB record of playing 2,131 consecutive games. Football: The San Francisco 49ers beat the San Diego Chargers 49-26 in Super Bowl XXIX. Basketball: The Houston Rockets swept the Orlando Magic 4 games to 0 to win the NBA Finals. The UCLA Bruins defeated the Arkansas Razorbacks 89-78 to win their record 11th NCAA men's basketball national championship. Hockey: The New Jersey Devils swept the Detroit Red Wings 4 games to 0 to win the Stanley Cup.

1996

BIRTHS: Actress Abigail Breslin (April 14) became the 4th youngest actress ever to be nominated for a Best Supporting Actress Academy Award for her role as Olive Hoover in the 2006 film *Little Miss Sunshine*. Tavi Gevinson (April 21) is a fashion blogger who created the online magazine *Rookie*, which publishes material ranging from pop culture and fashion advice to adolescent social issues and feminism. Zendaya Coleman (September 1) stars as the character Rocky Blue in the TV sitcom *Shake It Up* on the Disney Channel. Actress Hailee Steinfeld (December 11) received an Academy Award nomination for Best Supporting Actress for her role as Mattie Ross in the 2010 film *True Grit*.

ART: The 55-foot tall World Athletes Monument is carved in Indiana limestone and topped with 5 bronze statues supporting a globe. It was a gift from the Prince of Wales to the city of Atlanta, Georgia to celebrate the 1996 Summer Olympics.

FILM & TV: *The English Patient* won the Best Picture Academy Award as well as the Best Director Oscar for Anthony Minghella and the Best Supporting Actress Oscar for Juliette Binoche. Other top films were *Twister* starring Bill Paxton and Helen Hunt; *Independence Day* starring Will Smith; *The Rock* starring Sean Connery and Nicolas Cage; *101 Dalmatians* starring Glenn Close and Jeff Daniels; *Jerry Maguire* starring Tom Cruise and Renee Zellweger; and *The Nutty Professor* starring Eddie Murphy. Owen Wilson, Edward Norton, Emily Watson, Billy Crudup, and Julia Stiles made their film debuts. TV show premieres included *Everybody Loves Raymond*; *Spin City*; *3rd Rock from the Sun*; *Nash Bridges*; and *The Daily Show*.

INDUSTRY: The Dish Network provides satellite TV broadcast service to over 14 million U.S. customers. Jim Holland started the outdoor equipment online retailer Backcountry.com in his Huber City, Utah garage with $2,000.

LITERATURE: *Time* magazine political columnist Joe Klein's novel *Primary Colors* was originally published anonymously and spent 9 weeks at the top of the *New York Times* bestseller list.

MUSIC: Seal's "Kiss From a Rose" won the Song of the Year Grammy Award. Hootie & the Blowfish won Best New Artist. Other top songs were BoDeans "Closer to Free;" The Smashing Pumpkins' "1979;" Foo Fighters' "Big Me;" Jewel's "You Were Meant For Me;" and Beck's "Where It's At." Rapper Tupac Shakur died after being shot 4 times in Las Vegas, Nevada. His murder remains unsolved. The rock band KISS kicked off their reunion tour at Detroit's Tiger Stadium, the first time all 4 original members had performed together since 1979.

SPORTS: Baseball: The AL's New York Yankees defeated the NL's Atlanta Braves 4 games to 2 in the World Series. Football: The Dallas Cowboys beat the Pittsburgh Steelers 27-17 in Super Bowl XXX. Hockey: The Colorado Avalanche swept the Florida Panthers 4 games to 0 to win the Stanley Cup. Atlanta Summer Olympics: USA won the most medals (101) and the most gold medals (44).

THEATRE: Jonathan Larson's Broadway musical *Rent* ran for 12 years and 5,124 performances, winning the Pulitzer Prize for Drama and the Tony Award for Best Musical.

1997

BIRTHS: Chloe Grace Moretz (February 10) is a teen actress who received critical praise for her portrayal of Hit-Girl in the 2010 action film *Kick-Ass*. She also starred as Abby in the 2010 romantic horror film *Let Me In* and as Isabelle in Martin Scorsese's 2011 film *Hugo*. Swimmer Katie Ledecky (March 17) won the gold medal in the women's 800-meter freestyle with the 2nd fastest time ever. Rebecca Black (June 21) is a singer whose 2011 YouTube video for her single "Friday" received 167 million views and has been called 'the worst song ever' by many critics. Actress Bella Thorne (October 8) is best known for her role as CeCe Jones on Disney Channel's TV series *Shake It Up,* and has appeared in more than 60 TV commercials.

ART & ARCHITECTURE: The African American Civil War Memorial in Washington D.C. is a 9-foot tall bronze statue created by sculptor Ed Hamilton. It commemorates the 209,145 African-American soldiers and sailors who served in the Union Army during the U.S. Civil War. Los Angeles, California's Getty Center, designed by architect Richard Meier, specializes in displaying 20th century American photographs.

FILM & TV: *Titanic* won 11 of 14 Academy Award nominations including the Best Picture Oscar and the Best Director Oscar for James Cameron. It is the second-highest grossing film of all time (behind Cameron's *Avatar* in 2009), earning a worldwide total of $2.18 billion. Other top films were *Men in Black* starring Will Smith and Tommy Lee Jones; *The Lost World: Jurassic Park* starring Jeff Goldblum and Julianne Moore; *Air Force One* starring Harrison Ford and Gary Oldman; and *As Good as It Gets* starring Jack Nicholson (Best Actor Oscar) and Helen Hunt (Best Actress Oscar). Jennifer Garner, Orlando Bloom, Aaron Eckhart, and Katie Holmes made their film debuts. TV show premieres included *King of the Hill; Ally McBeal; South Park; Dharma & Greg;* and *Buffy the Vampire Slayer.*

INDUSTRY: Netflix provides rental DVDs by mail and on-demand Internet streaming media to over 23 million U.S. subscribers. Lionsgate Films is the largest and most successful independent film studio in North America.

LITERATURE: Works published include Mitch Albom's *Tuesdays with Morrie;* Candace Bushnell's *Sex and the City;* Charles Frazier's *Cold Mountain;* and J.K. Rowling's *Harry Potter and the Philosopher's Stone.*

MUSIC: Eric Clapton's "Change the World" won the Song of the Year Grammy Award. LeAnn Rimes won Best New Artist. Other top songs were Hanson's "MMMBop," Sean Combs' "I'll Be Missing You," Matchbox Twenty's "3 A.M.," and Elton John's "Candle in the Wind 1997." With over 34 million copies worldwide, Shania Twain's *Come on Over* is the biggest selling album in country music history and the biggest selling album by any female artist.

SPORTS: Baseball: The NL's Florida Marlins defeated the AL's Cleveland Indians 4 games to 3 in the World Series. Football: The Green Bay Packers beat the New England Patriots 35-21 in Super Bowl XXXI. Basketball: The Houston Comets defeated the New York Liberty 65-51 in the first Women's National Basketball Association championship. Golf: Tiger Woods became the world's number one ranked golfer in only his 42nd week as a professional.

THEATRE: The Broadway musical *The Lion King* won the Tony Award for Best Musical. Still running with over 5,350 performances and more than $850 million in receipts, it is the highest grossing Broadway show of all time.

1998

BIRTHS: Actress Kerris Dorsey (January 9) played Paige Whedon on the TV series *Brothers & Sisters* from 2006 to 2011. She also portrayed Casey Beane, daughter of Billy Beane (played by Brad Pitt), in the 2011 film *Moneyball*. Ariel Winter (January 28) is best known for her role as Alex Dunphy on the ABC TV series *Modern Family*. Jaden Smith (July 8) is the son of actors Will Smith and Jada Pinkett Smith. He starred with Jackie Chan in the 2010 film *The Karate Kid*, a remake of the 1984 film. Rico Rodriguez (July 31) plays Manny Delgado on the ABC TV series *Modern Family*.

ART & ARCHITECTURE: Sculptor Susan Luery's *Babe's Dream* is a bronze statue of baseball legend Babe Ruth that stands outside Oriole Park at Camden Yards in Baltimore, Maryland. The Bellagio Hotel and Casino on the Las Vegas Strip is famous for its 'Fountains of Bellagio,' a free dancing water show synchronized to music in the 8-acre lake in front of the hotel.

FILM & TV: *Shakespeare in Love* won the Best Picture Academy Award as well as the Best Actress Oscar for Gwyneth Paltrow and the Best Supporting Actress Oscar for Judi Dench. Other top films were *Armageddon* starring Bruce Willis and Ben Affleck; Steven Spielberg's (Best Director Oscar) *Saving Private Ryan* starring Tom Hanks; *There's Something About Mary* starring Ben Stiller and Cameron Diaz; *Godzilla* starring Matthew Broderick; *Dr. Doolittle* starring Eddie Murphy; and Disney's *Mulan*. Josh Hartnett, Eva Mendes, Jason Segel, and Lindsay Lohan made their film debuts. TV show premieres included *That 70s Show; Dawson's Creek; Sex and the City; Will and Grace; Teletubbies; The King of Queens;* and *Whose Line Is It Anyway?*

INDUSTRY: Google was founded in Menlo Park, California and today is the number one visited Internet website, processing more than 1 billion search requests every day. Rapper Sean Combs founded the clothing and fragrance company Sean John, which now generates revenues of over $100 million annually. FunKo produces over 1,000 different licensed bobblehead toys.

LITERATURE: Travel writer Bill Bryson's *A Walk in the Woods* describes his attempt to hike the entire Appalachian Trail with his friend.

MUSIC: Shawn Colvin's "Sunny Came Home" won the Song of the Year Grammy Award. Paula Cole won Best New Artist. Other top songs were Goo Goo Dolls' "Iris;" Aerosmith's "I Don't Want to Miss a Thing;" Madonna's "Ray of Light;" Cher's "Believe;" Semisonic's "Closing Time;" Shania Twain's You're Still the One;" and Run D.M.C.'s "It's Like That."

SPORTS: Baseball: The AL's New York Yankees swept the NL's San Diego Padres 4 games to 0 in the World Series. Football: The Denver Broncos beat the Green Bay Packers 31-24 in Super Bowl XXXII. The University of Tennessee Volunteers won college football's first Bowl Championship Series (BCS) and became national champions by defeating the Florida State University Seminoles 23-16 in the Fiesta Bowl in Tempe, Arizona. Hockey: The Detroit Red Wings swept the Washington Capitals 4 games to 0 to win the Stanley Cup. Women played hockey for the first time in Olympic history, with the USA winning the gold medal 3-1 over Canada. Motor Racing: After 19 years of coming up short, Dale Earnhardt won the only Daytona 500 race title of his career. Dogsled Racing: Jeff King won the 3rd of his 4 Iditarod Trail Sled Dog Race Championships with lead dogs Red and Rocket.

1999

BIRTHS: Karan Brar (January 18) is an actor best known for his role as Chirag Gupta in the *Diary of a Wimpy Kid* film series. He also stars as Ravi Ross on the Disney Channel's comedy series *Jessie.* Actor Cameron Boyce (May 28) has appeared in the films *Grown Ups, Eagle Eye,* and *Mirrors.* Bailee Madison (October 15) is an actress who portrayed Mary Belle Aarons in the 2007 film *Bridge to Terabithia.* She had her first leading role in the 2011 horror film, *Don't Be Afraid of the Dark.* Kiernan Shipka (November 10) has played the role of Sally Draper, daughter of Don and Betty Draper on the AMC TV series *Mad Men* since 2007.

FILM & TV: *American Beauty* won the Best Picture Academy Award as well as the Best Director Oscar for Sam Mendes and the Best Actor Oscar for Kevin Spacey. Other top films were *The Sixth Sense* starring Bruce Willis and Hayley Joel Osment; *Star Wars Episode 1: The Phantom Menace* starring Liam Neeson, Ewan McGregor, and Natalie Portman; *The Matrix* starring Keanu Reeves and Laurence Fishburne; *Notting Hill* starring Julia Roberts and Hugh Grant; *The Mummy* starring Brendan Fraser and Rachel Weisz; and Disney's *Tarzan.* James Franco, Amy Adams, Hugh Jackman, Zooey Deschanel, Ashton Kutcher, and Kristen Stewart made their film debuts. TV show premieres included *The Sopranos; The West Wing; Family Guy; Who Want to Be a Millionaire; SpongeBob SquarePants;* and *Futurama.*

INDUSTRY: The digital video recorder TiVo records digital TV programs onto a hard disc allowing users to watch what they want, anytime. Monster.com is the world's largest online job search engine featuring more than 1 million job postings at any time and 63 million job seekers per month. Napster's peer-to-peer music and movie file sharing service led to many copyright violations and was eventually shut down by court order.

MUSIC: Celine Dion's "My Heart Will Go On" won the Song of the Year Grammy Award. Lauryn Hill won Best New Artist. Other top songs were Britney Spears' "...Baby One More Time;" TLC's "No Scrubs;" Smash Mouth's "All Star;" Mariah Carey's "Heartbreaker;" Sugar Ray's "Every Morning;" Ricky Martin's "Livin' la Vida Loca;" Eminem's "My Name Is;" and Backstreet Boys' "I Want It That Way." The music rights management company BMI announced the 100 all time most played songs on American radio. The top 10: 1. The Righteous Brothers' "You've Lost That Loving Feeling." 2. The Association's "Never My Love." 3. The Beatles' "Yesterday." 4. Ben E. King's "Stand By Me." 5. Frankie Valli's "Can't Take My Eyes Off You." 6. Otis Redding's "(Sittin' On) The Dock of the Bay." 7. Simon & Garfunkel's "Mrs. Robinson." 8. The Four Tops' "Baby I Need Your Loving." 9. The Cascades' "Rhythm of the Rain." 10. Ray Charles' "Georgia on my Mind."

SPORTS: Baseball: The AL's New York Yankees swept the NL's Atlanta Braves 4 games to 0 in the World Series. Football: The Denver Broncos beat the Atlanta Falcons 34-19 in Super Bowl XXXIII. Legendary Chicago Bears running back Walter Payton died at the age of 45 from a rare form of liver cancer. Basketball: The San Antonio Spurs won their first NBA Finals championship, defeating the New York Knicks 4 games to 1. Hockey: The Dallas Stars beat the Buffalo Sabres 4 games to 2 to win the Stanley Cup. Golf: Professional golfer Payne Stewart died in an airplane crash 4 months after winning the U.S. Open Golf Championship.

Made in the USA
Las Vegas, NV
03 November 2022